LEAD GUITAR 101

By Kirk Tatnall

To access audio visit:
www.halleonard.com/mylibrary

Enter Code
4668-9752-3368-6824

ISBN 978-1-5400-2030-7

HAL•LEONARD®

Visit Hal Leonard Online at
www.halleonard.com

Contact us:
Hal Leonard
7777 West Bluemound Road
Milwaukee, WI 53213
Email: info@halleonard.com

In Europe, contact:
Hal Leonard Europe Limited
Distribution Centre, Newmarket Road
Bury St Edmunds, Suffolk, IP33 3YB
Email: info@halleonardeurope.com

In Australia, contact:
Hal Leonard Australia Pty. Ltd.
4 Lentara Court
Cheltenham, Victoria, 3192 Australia
Email: info@halleonard.com.au

CONTENTS

INTRODUCTION

Welcome to *Lead Guitar 101*. The goal of this book is to present a clear path to learning the essential scale fingerings needed for playing lead guitar in the most popular guitar keys. As you travel along this path, you will learn to create musical phrases while simultaneously developing a large vocabulary of rhythms to improvise with.

Most guitarists begin their journey into playing lead guitar by being presented with a scale fingering diagram. The real challenge begins with the question "How do I turn this into music?" Since the art of making music is marrying melodies to rhythms, it makes sense to apply rhythms to scale practice right from the start. Doing so has three main benefits:

Enjoyable Practice Sessions: The instant you add a rhythm to a scale pattern, the result renders actual music! Instead of endlessly running up and down scale fingerings like reciting the alphabet, you will practice being musical.

Rhythmic Vocabulary Development: When scales and melodic patterns are practiced with rhythms applied, the student will get a feel for how rhythm patterns influence a melody, and will develop the ability to improvise them without consciously counting.

Increased Technical Ability: When triplets and sixteenth notes are introduced into scale passages, it naturally requires that certain combinations of notes get played faster than others. As you shift the faster rhythms to each beat of a measure, you will end up playing different combinations of notes faster than you could play the entire passage at one speed. The result is that your technical ability will develop faster than it would by simply going up and down scales with one rhythm.

While there are many scale fingerings available across the neck of the guitar, a study of guitar solos reveals that the majority of them are based around their corresponding barre chords and the diagonal fingerings that shift through the middle of them. Practicing this book will enable you to spot these patterns immediately on the fretboard and give you a clear direction to making music with them.

Chapter 1: Pentatonic Fingering 1

Shown below are the two most popular fingerings for the pentatonic scale. The alternate fingering puts the strongest fingers on the most commonly bent notes, which are the highest notes on strings one, two, and three. You may find yourself switching between fingerings situationally. Start by simply playing up and down the patterns to familiarize yourself with them.

Pentatonic Fingering 1

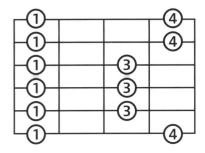

Alternate Fingering

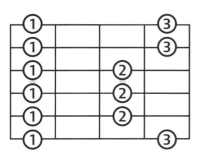

Our next step is to begin hearing the two main sounds obtained from the pentatonic scale, which are major and minor. A great way to do so is to strum the chord shape contained within the scale, and then play the scale from root to root. The diamonds in the diagrams below are there to help you visualize the open G chord shape and are not played in these examples. Since the full G chord is hard to move around the neck, the two abbreviated chords below are often used.

C Chord Played With the Fourth Finger on the Sixth String
(Sixth-String-Root Open G Chord Shape)

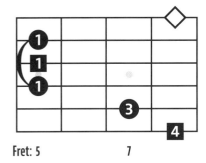

Fret: 5   7

C Chord Played With the Fourth Finger on the First String
(First-String-Root Open G Chord Shape)

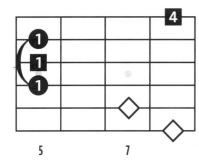

5   7

Notice where the notes of the chord are located within the scale.

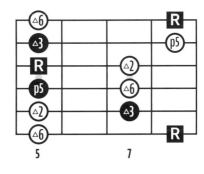

5   7

The labels in the diagram indicate the scale degree as related to the major scale and are used throughout this book. Instead of "Do, Re, Me" think "Root, Two, Three."

triangle = major interval

flat = minor interval

p = perfect interval

Consult a music theory book for further study.

As you play the following exercise, observe the major pentatonic sound (happy) created by starting from and emphasizing the C root notes.

Track 1

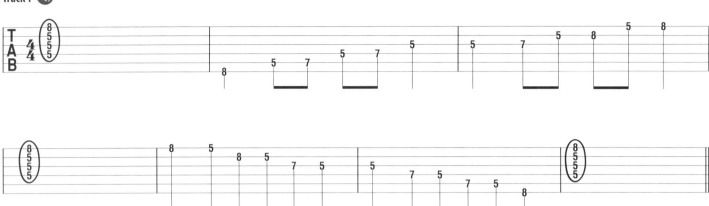

The next important sound obtained from our scale is the minor pentatonic. By changing the starting note of the scale from C to A, or from the root to the 6th step, the minor sound and chord are produced. For more in-depth study you may want to consult a music theory book, but for now we will simply observe how different the scale sounds when started from the first finger rather than the fourth. Strum the chord, and then play the scale starting from your first finger.

Am Chord Played with the First Finger on the Sixth String
(Sixth-String-Root Open Em Chord Shape)

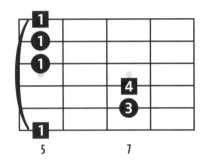

Am Pentatonic Fingering 1
(Line Your First Finger Up on the Root)

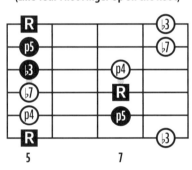

As you play the following exercise, observe the minor pentatonic sound (serious or sad) created by starting from and emphasizing the A root notes.

Track 2

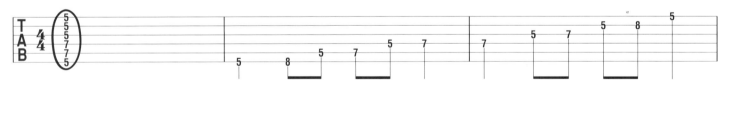

To summarize what we have learned so far, line the root of the scale up on your fourth finger to sound major, and from your first finger to sound minor.

Pentatonic Fingering 1 in the Five Most Popular Guitar Keys

Use the charts below to move the pentatonic scale around the fretboard and, as you do, observe how the fingering looks and feels when the fret spacing changes. Use the black dots to visualize the chord shape within the scale pattern. Refer back to this page as necessary when moving cell exercises to new keys.

C Major Pentatonic
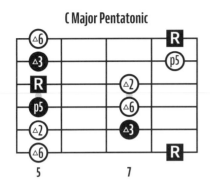

C Minor Pentatonic
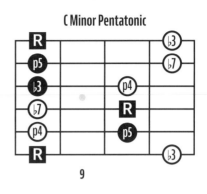

A Major Pentatonic
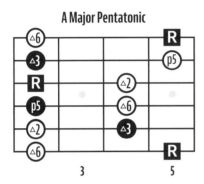

A Minor Pentatonic
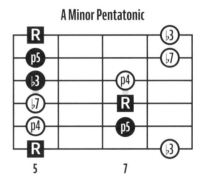

G Major Pentatonic
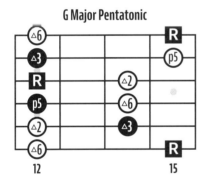

G Minor Pentatonic
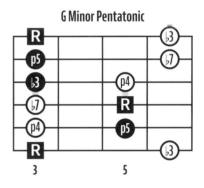

E Major Pentatonic
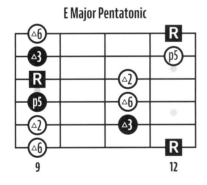

E Minor Pentatonic
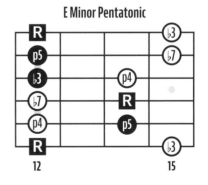

D Major Pentatonic
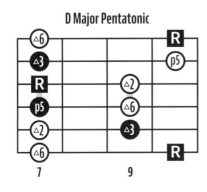

D Minor Pentatonic
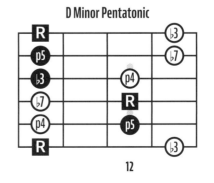

How to Practice This Book

These next pages are very important as they lay the groundwork on how this book is used. Take the time to absorb these ideas so you can apply them to the pages that follow. For each cell exercise, we will apply a simple three-step practice method.

Step 1: Play the Phrase and Apply a Rhythm

For each exercise, first learn the pattern as written in straight eighth notes. After you can comfortably play the pattern, then apply a rhythm to it—practice rhythms are located on the bottom of the exercise pages. The first four rhythms on each page have a corresponding audio track and are used as the basis for each page's exercise. You will also find more rhythms at the back of the book.

Shown below are examples of the same series of notes played with different rhythms. Take note of how the rhythms impart a distinctive quality and transform it from being just an exercise into a unique musical phrase. The same series of notes can sound totally different when you change up the rhythms!

Track 3

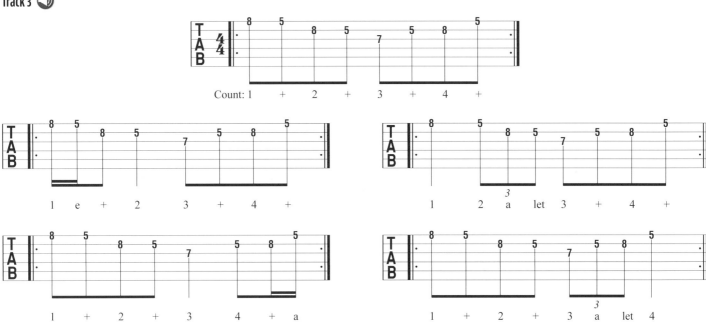

Step 2: Use the Blueprint to Change Keys

To the right of each phrase you will find the phrase blueprint. The "X's" show which string the note is played on and the number directly under it shows which finger is used on the note. After playing the exercise as written, use the blueprint, along with the scale diagrams near the beginning of the chapter, to move the example along the neck into different keys. Observe how, in the examples below, you are simply moving the same fingering along the fretboard.

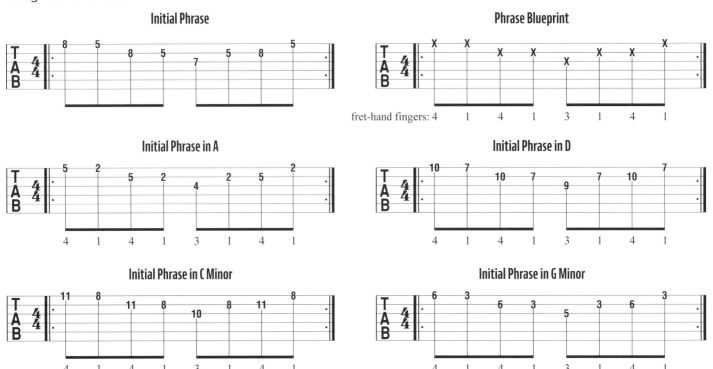

Step 3: Improvise Using a Set Rhythm Pattern

Once you've established your key and have played the exercise several times with your chosen rhythm pattern, it's time to experiment with changing the notes on the fly while using the same rhythm pattern. By improvising with the same rhythm pattern, a couple of important things happen.

1. Playing a defined rhythm takes pressure off of the beginning improviser, who is now free to change the notes at will without having to improvise the rhythm simultaneously. Doing this repeatedly embeds rhythms into your vocabulary.

2. There are few things the ear likes more than a repeated rhythm pattern. The repeated rhythm figure itself provides an instant theme to the improvisation.

Shown below are some ideas to help get you started. Take them and apply them to various examples in the book. Also observe how they are used in the example solos at the end of each chapter. If these seem difficult, try practicing some cell exercises first and come back to these ideas later.

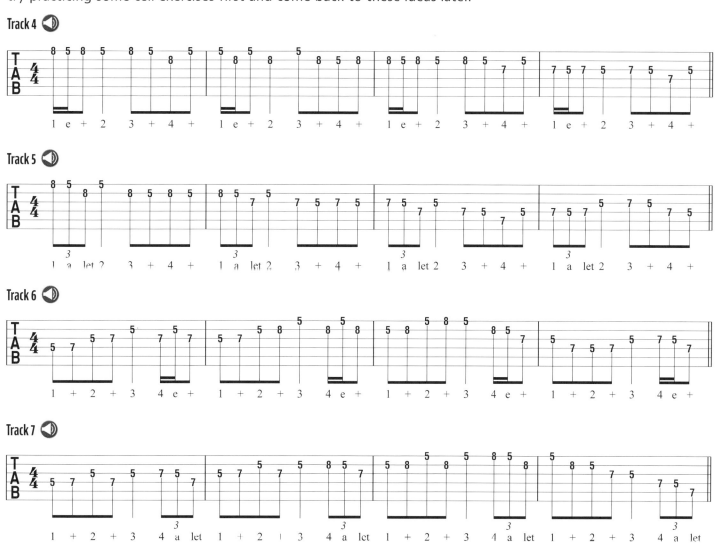

About Using the Audio

The accompanying audio tracks and audio player provided at **www.halleonard.com/mylibrary** are an absolutely essential part of working with this book. The audio player lets you adjust the tempo and change the key of the track to fit your needs. Here are some tips on getting maximum benefit from them.

1. **Change the speed to fit your experience level:** Even though the backing tracks used for the book are at slow to moderate tempos, they are most often too fast when just beginning. There is no such thing as going too slow! Playing the examples accurately and in time are the priority. Use the original tempo as a real world goal to shoot for.

2. **Change the key of the recording:** The keys of all of the recorded examples can be moved up or down in half steps. Want to play a blues in B♭? Shift Track 399, which is a C blues, down two half steps and move your scale fingering down two frets. The ability to easily change keys really increases the benefits of the audio.

3. **Remove the guide track:** When you sing along with your favorite song, it is easier to find your pitch because you can match the original singer. The same holds true with the audio for this book. First play the exercises with the audio, then play them with the corresponding backing track and improvise with the rhythm pattern you are working on. It's the equivalent of taking the training wheels off the bike.

Descending Four-Note Cells Played on the Upper Strings

The term "four-note cell" refers to the grouping of notes we play stepwise up or down the scale. Each pattern goes down four notes and then back up four notes, returning you to the starting pitch when you repeat. The practice method for the first cell is mapped out on page 8.

The headings above each example describe the rhythm and key heard in the corresponding audio track. For example, Track 13 features the displayed cell moved to C minor and played with Rhythm 2, which is on the bottom of this page. Feel free to go back and review if necessary.

First play the following phrases as written, then apply a rhythm from below or from the Appendix. Use the phrase blueprints, scale diagrams, and corresponding audio tracks to change keys. Continue playing the rhythm and improvise your note choices using these backing tracks: C Major Backing Track 382 for Rhythm 1, C Blues Backing Track 399 for Rhythm 2, E Major Backing Track 383 for Rhythm 3, and G Blues Backing Track 400 for Rhythm 4.

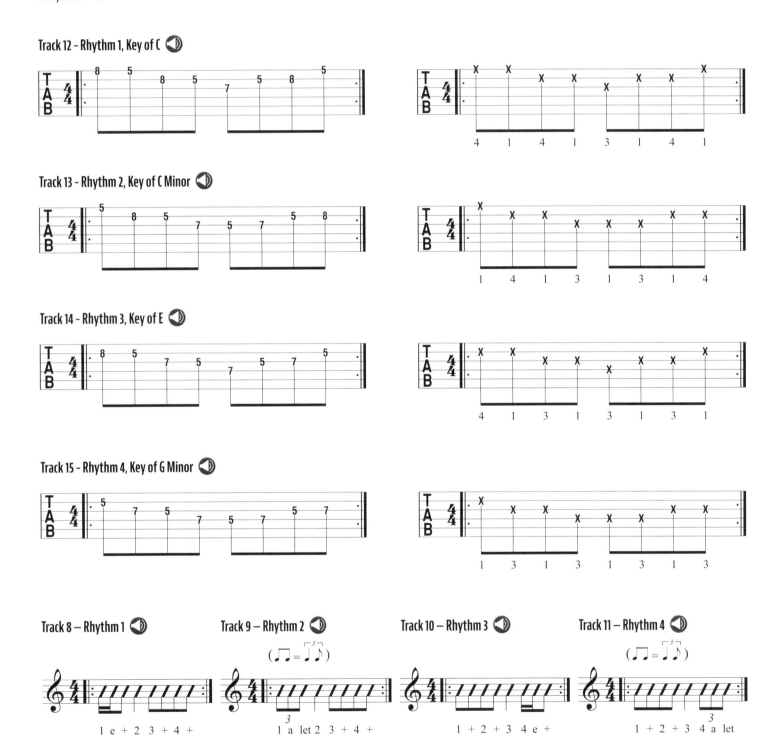

Ascending Four-Note Cells Played on the Upper Strings

By turning the same phrase around and ascending first, we can create a whole different feel with the same notes.

First play the following phrases as written, then apply a rhythm from below or from the Appendix. Use the phrase blueprints, scale diagrams, and corresponding audio tracks to change keys. Continue playing the rhythm and improvise your note choices using these backing tracks: C Major Backing Track 382 for Rhythm 1, C Blues Backing Track 399 for Rhythm 2, E Major Backing Track 383 for Rhythm 3, and G Blues Backing Track 400 for Rhythm 4.

Track 16 - Rhythm 1, Key of C

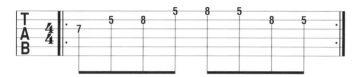
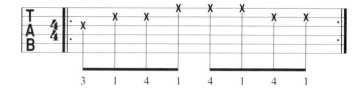

Track 17 - Rhythm 2, Key of C Minor

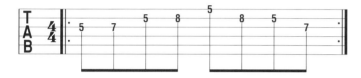
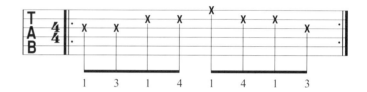

Track 18 - Rhythm 3, Key of E

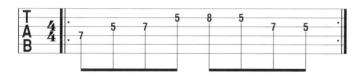
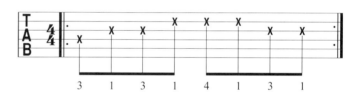

Track 19 - Rhythm 4, Key of G Minor

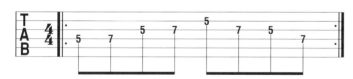
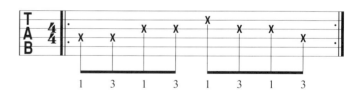

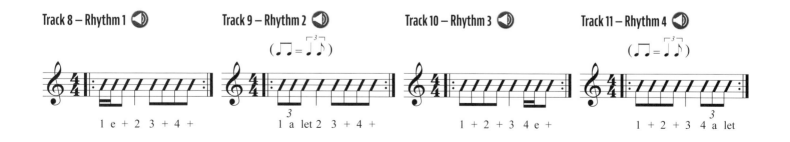

Practice Session Strategies

One of the key factors in absorbing new material is to have a good game plan. When you are just beginning, it may take all of your energy to play a few cell exercises, but as you progress you will be able to get through more things in one practice session. As this happens you may want to practice the book in a more modular kind of way.

One of the easiest and most efficient ways to practice this book is to go through each chapter playing one key and rhythm at a time. Each chapter contains audio examples in four keys, each with its own rhythm pattern. Follow this detailed explanation using Chapter 1 as an example:

1. Decide which key you will play in this practice session. For example, let's pick C minor and the second cell of each page.

2. Start by playing the second cell on page 13 as written, then use the phrase blueprint and scale diagrams to move the cell to C minor. In this case, we'll move the scale fingering to fret 8.

3. Put on Track 21, which demonstrates the cell played in C minor with Rhythm 2, and try to play along with it. If you need to, adjust the playback speed with the audio player at **www.halleonard.com/mylibrary**. There is no such thing as "too slow," only the right speed for your current ability. Playing it correctly and in time is the most important thing!

4. After you've absorbed the rhythm pattern fully, use Track 399 and play the pattern without Track 21 as your guide. Again, set the speed to your ability.

5. Continue playing the rhythm pattern but improvise your note choices using only the notes of the scale fingering you are learning. You may find this difficult or unnerving at first, but like anything, it can be practiced.

6. Turn to page 11 and repeat the process with the second cell and Track 17. Then remove the guide and play it with Track 399 again. Next, change the notes freely while playing the same rhythm.

7. Repeat the process, playing the second cell on pages 10 and 14, this time emphasizing the lower notes of the scale.

8. Work the rhythm through the entire scale fingering using the exercises on pages 16 and 17. This will develop your ability to create longer phrases. Learn the exercise as written with straight eighth notes first before applying the rhythm. At this point, you may be able to skip right to using the blueprint at the 8th fret. Use Tracks 29 and 33 to aid in the process.

9. Work through Solo 2 on page 18, using Track 37. Try learning the solo two measures at a time before attempting the whole thing.

10. Improvise freely using Track 399 as your backing track. By this time, chances are very high that Rhythm 2 will be a large part of your solo! By practicing this way, you are developing your vocabulary of rhythms and learning to improvise while learning your scale fingerings. After working with one key and rhythm throughout your practice session, you will naturally internalize both the rhythm and the fingering. Even if you only use the first four rhythms in each chapter, you will quickly develop a rhythmic vocabulary as you progress through the book.

Using this method really focuses on absorbing and using each rhythm pattern and is the recommended way to start. As the material becomes more familiar, you can invent your own ways to practice, as varying your routine can keep things exciting and help you learn faster. For example, you could try playing and improvising in all four keys presented on one page before turning to the next. Doing so incorporates four different rhythms, keys, and groove environments in one practice session. Eventually, you will be able to mix and match cells, rhythms, keys, and backing tracks any way you would like!

Descending Four-Note Cells Played on the Lower Strings

The following phrases emphasize the lower portion of the scale fingering.

First play the following phrases as written, then apply a rhythm from below or from the Appendix. Use the phrase blueprints, scale diagrams, and corresponding audio tracks to change keys. Continue playing the rhythm and improvise your note choices using these backing tracks: C Major Backing Track 382 for Rhythm 1, C Blues Backing Track 399 for Rhythm 2, E Major Backing Track 383 for Rhythm 3, and G Blues Backing Track 400 for Rhythm 4.

Track 20 – Rhythm 1, Key of C

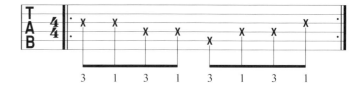

Track 21 – Rhythm 2, Key of C Minor

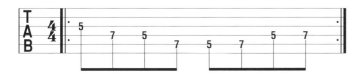
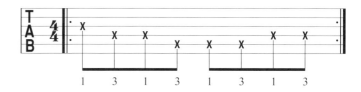

Track 22 – Rhythm 3, Key of E

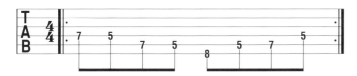
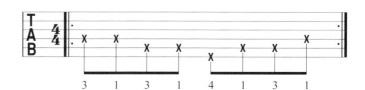

Track 23 – Rhythm 4, Key of G Minor

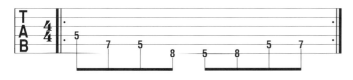
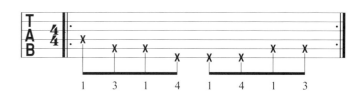

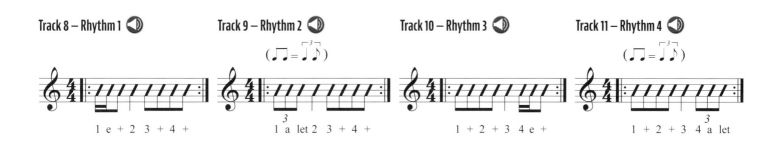

Ascending Four-Note Cells Played on the Lower Strings

Again, switching the direction of the line creates a new feel for the patterns.

First play the following phrases as written, then apply a rhythm from below or from the Appendix. Use the phrase blueprints, scale diagrams, and corresponding audio tracks to change keys. Continue playing the rhythm and improvise your note choices using these backing tracks: C Major Backing Track 382 for Rhythm 1, C Blues Backing Track 399 for Rhythm 2, E Major Backing Track 383 for Rhythm 3, and G Blues Backing Track 400 for Rhythm 4.

Track 24 - Rhythm 1, Key of C

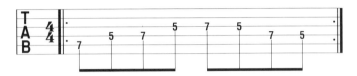
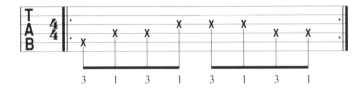

Track 25 - Rhythm 2, Key of C Minor

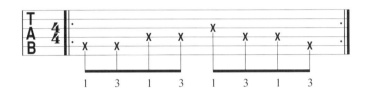

Track 26 - Rhythm 3, Key of E

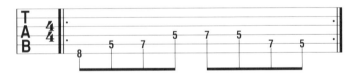
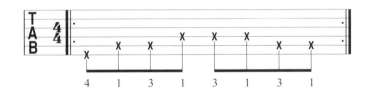

Track 27 - Rhythm 4, Key of G Minor

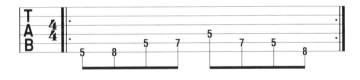
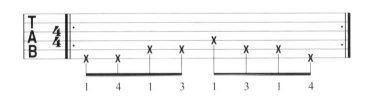

Track 8 – Rhythm 1   Track 9 – Rhythm 2   Track 10 – Rhythm 3   Track 11 – Rhythm 4

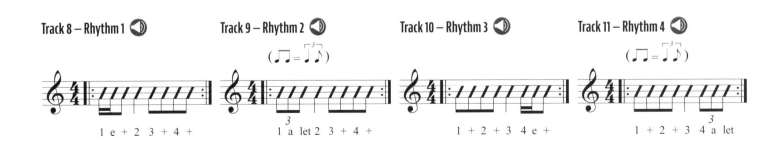

Ideas for Improvising with Rhythms

If you are finding that letting go of the cell pattern and improvising with a rhythm is an unnerving experience, don't worry. You are not alone! Remember that if you are playing the correct scale there are no wrong notes. It is simply a matter of arranging notes into phrases that you like and then stringing them together. The process is very much like speaking. To get a point across we pull words out of our vocabulary and arrange them as needed. Of course this takes time to develop, and because we are speaking with each other all the time we practice it constantly. Making melodies is really no different.

Let's take a look at some ideas to get you started. While experimenting with the examples below, you may want to try repeating each measure several times. Doing so allows you to absorb the idea before stringing it together with the next measure.

Repeat a Note: While playing up or down a scale, simply find a note you like and play it more than once.

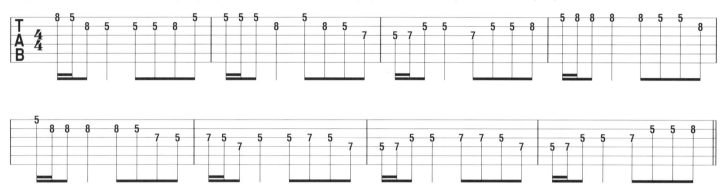

Two-Note Phrases: Much like the above example, take two notes and repeat them in any fashion you'd like. Try inserting these two-note pairs in between scale patterns that just go up and down. Also try putting different two-note pairs next to each other.

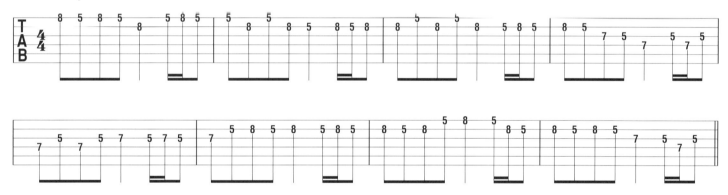

Three-Note Phrases: Try repeating a three-note phrase and inserting it next to standard "up and down the scale"-type movement.

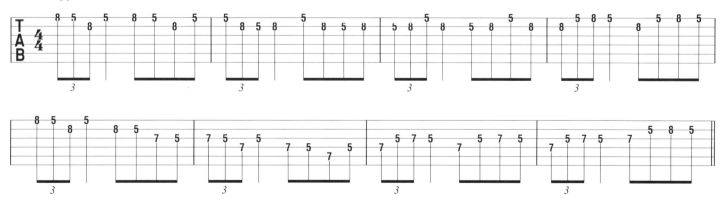

As you continue the cell exercises in this chapter, consciously apply one-, two-, and three-note phrases to step 3 of the practice method.

Descending Four-Note Cells Connected

In the following example, all of the cells you've practiced already are chained together into one long phrase. Mastering this phrase will help you create longer lines that cover more of the scale fingering. Take notice of how you repeat the ending note of each measure and shift the cell one note further down the scale each time.

Track 28 - Rhythm 1, Key of C

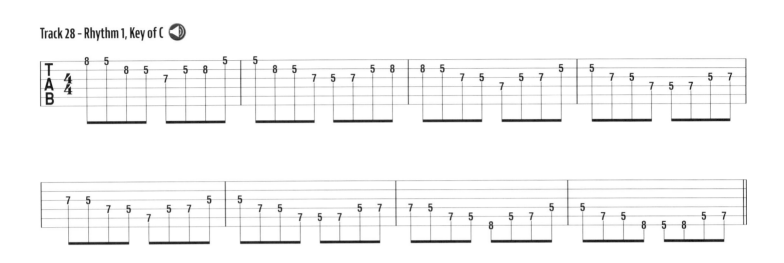

When you can play the above exercise as written, use the blueprint below to change keys. Then use C Major Backing Track 382 for Rhythm 1, C Blues Backing Track 399 for Rhythm 2, E Major Backing Track 383 for Rhythm 3, and G Blues Backing Track 400 for Rhythm 4. More rhythms can be found in the Appendix.

Track 29 - Rhythm 2, Key of C Minor   Track 30 - Rhythm 3, Key of E   Track 31 - Rhythm 4, Key of G Minor

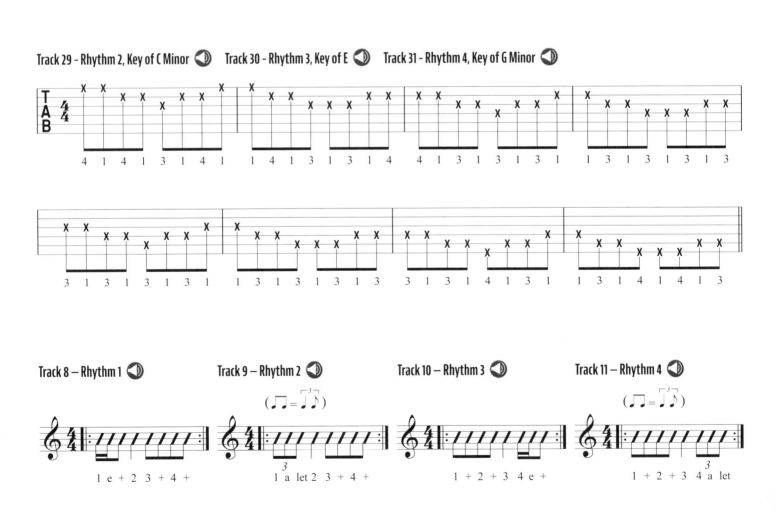

Ascending Four-Note Cells Connected

Reversing the direction will enable you to play ascending lines as well. Once again, repeating the ending note of each measure advances you one note at a time through the scale pattern. As you get a feel for this pattern, you can shift your focus from reading to simply playing.

Track 32 - Rhythm 1, Key of C

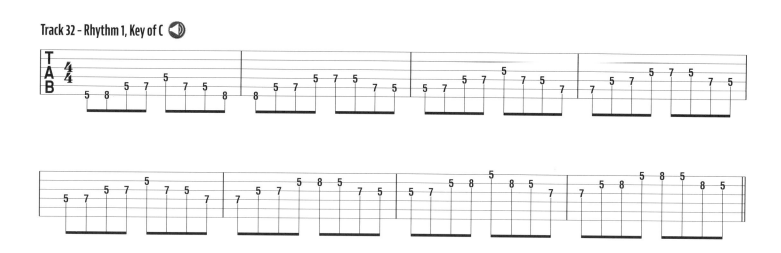

When you can play the above exercise as written, use the blueprint below to change keys. Then use C Major Backing Track 382 for Rhythm 1, C Blues Backing Track 399 for Rhythm 2, E Major Backing Track 383 for Rhythm 3, and G Blues Backing Track 400 for Rhythm 4. More rhythms can be found in the Appendix.

Track 33 - Rhythm 2, Key of C Minor   Track 34 - Rhythm 3, Key of E   Track 35 - Rhythm 4, Key of G Minor

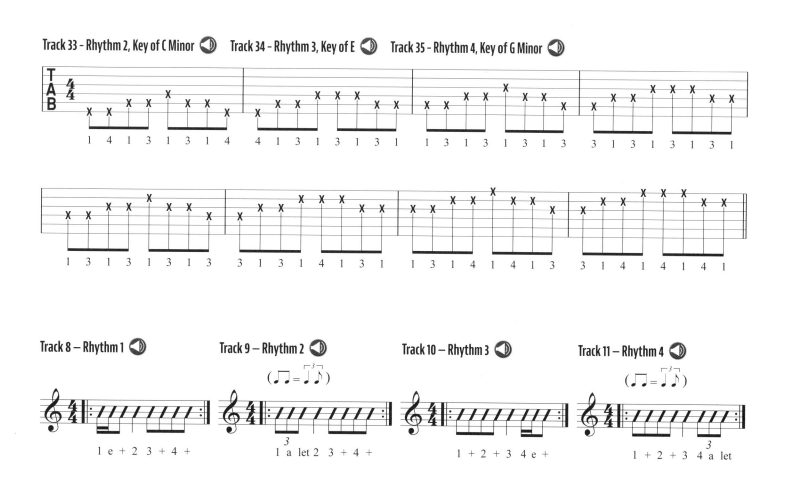

A very important part of making musical phrases is learning where to put a pause. This is sometimes described as "taking a breath" or "putting the period at the end of a sentence." Playing a rhythm pattern repeatedly is a great device, but much like speaking, you also need to take breaks in order for the listener to digest the information.

The sample solos in this book demonstrate how to do this by simply adding a half note on beat 3 or beat 1 every other measure. This creates a two-measure phrase that allows for a breath in the music. Learn each solo by playing each two-measure phrase individually, and then string them together one line at a time until you can play the entire solo.

Solo 1: Two-Measure Phrases Using C Major Fingering 1

Track 36   Backing Track 382

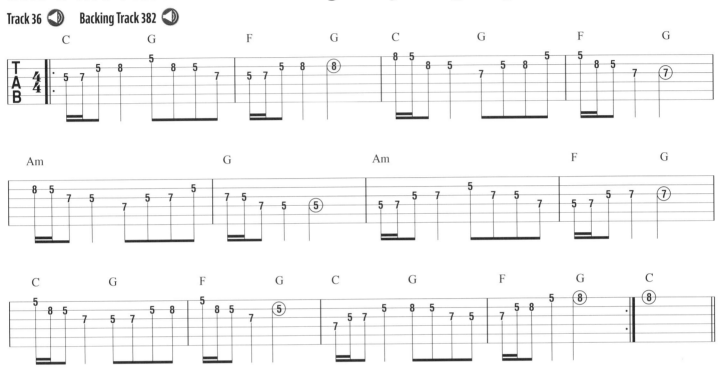

Solo 2: Two-Measure Phrases Using C Minor Fingering 1

Track 37   Backing Track 399

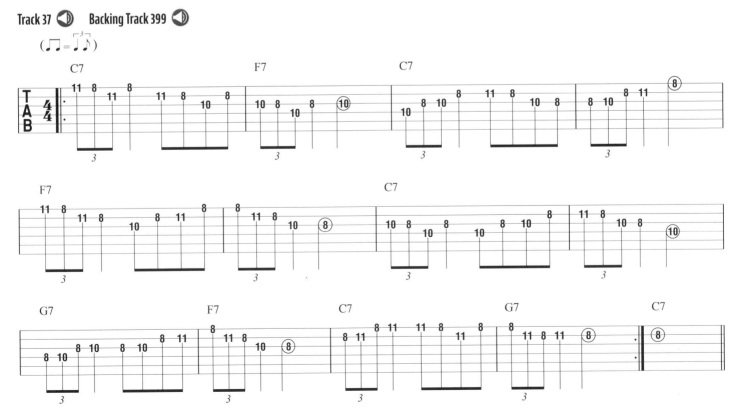

Solo 3: Two-Measure Phrases Using E Major Fingering 1

Track 38 ♪♪♪ Backing Track 383 ♪♪♪

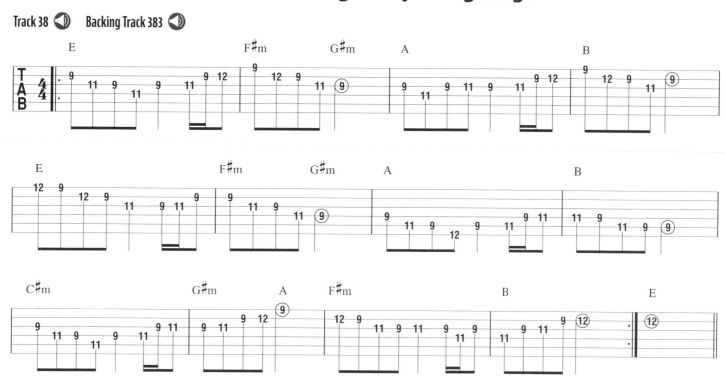

Solo 4: Two-Measure Phrases Using G Minor Fingering 1

Track 39 ♪♪♪ Backing Track 400 ♪♪♪

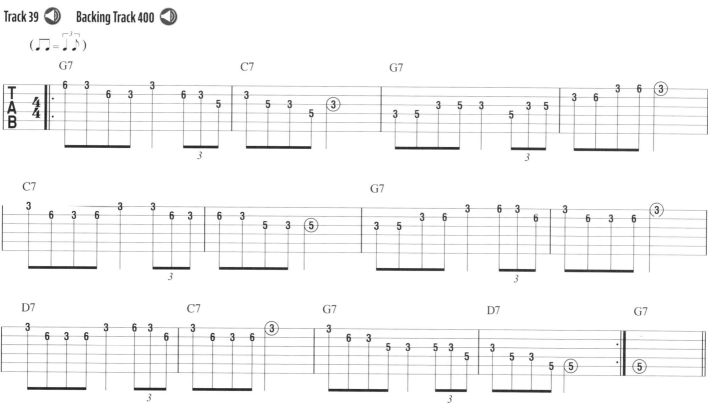

Chapter 2: Diagonal Pentatonic 1

Diagonal Pentatonic 1 is a pattern that is created by sliding through three of the five pentatonic positions and gets it name from the way it lays across the fretboard. This shape is a great asset because of the very musical slides between the 2nd and 3rd degrees of the major pentatonic, or the 4th and 5th degrees of the minor pentatonic, depending on how you are using the scale.

There are many uses for all five of the pentatonic positions, but a study of guitar solos will reveal that fingerings 2 and 5 are used most when slid into from Fingering 1. Study the diagrams below and observe the black dots. They are the notes in common with our new fingering. As you try the diagonal fingering be aware of where you are moving through each of the positions.

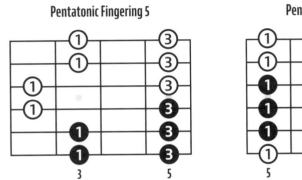

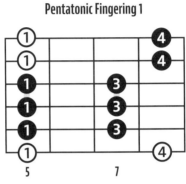

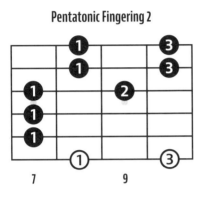

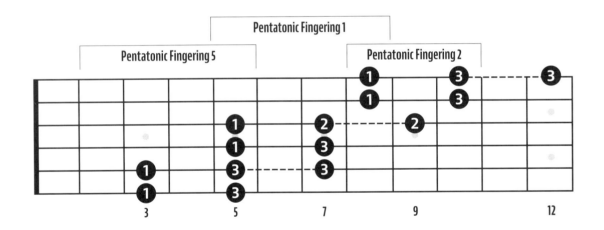

Visualizing Diagonal Pentatonic 1

A key component to "seeing" Diagonal Pentatonic 1 on the fretboard is visualizing the three symmetrical five-note groupings. The white note markers on strings 3 and 4 visually make each five-note grouping stand out. Play the following exercises while studying the diagrams. Take special care to use your second finger where indicated.

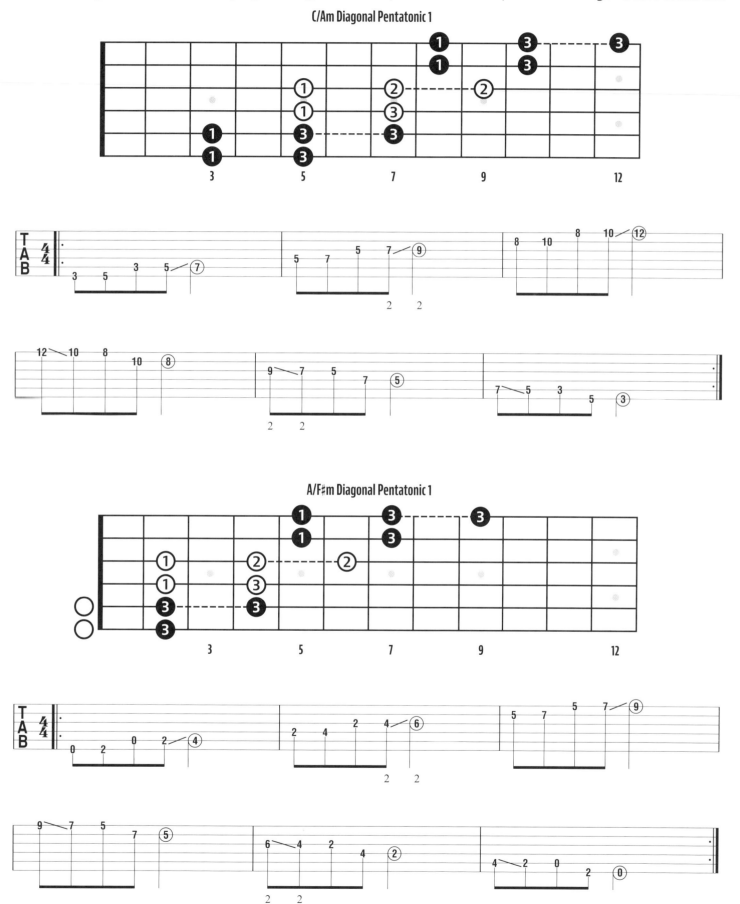

C/Am Diagonal Pentatonic 1

A/F♯m Diagonal Pentatonic 1

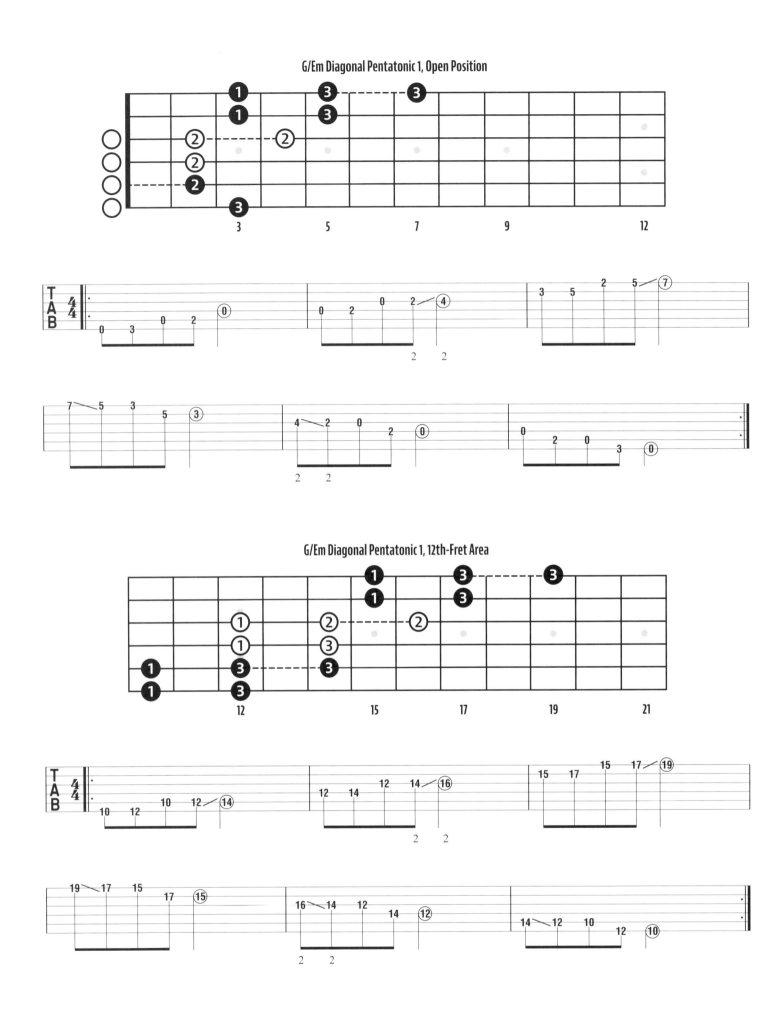

G/Em Diagonal Pentatonic 1, Open Position

G/Em Diagonal Pentatonic 1, 12th-Fret Area

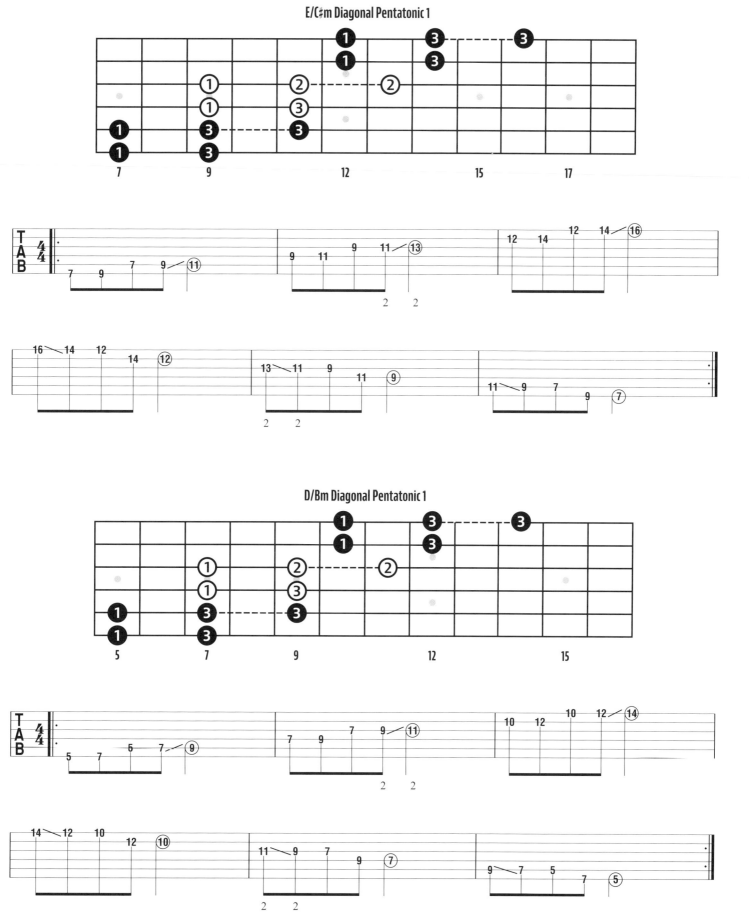

Diagonal Pentatonic 1 in the Key of C/Am

Use the diagrams below to see where our new fingering intersects with Pentatonic Fingering 1, and how the notes are used as major or minor.

Pentatonic Fingering 1, Sixth-String Roots

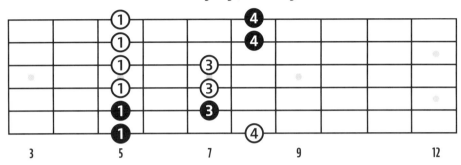

Diagonal Pentatonic 1, Travels Through Fingering 1

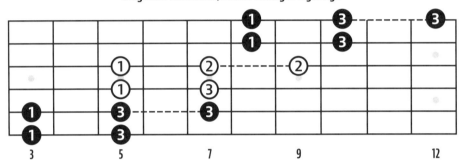

Diagonal Pentatonic 1, Intervals Shown as C Major

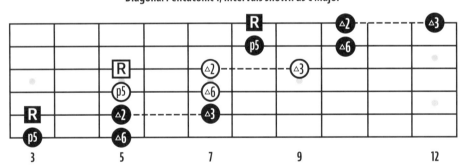

Diagonal Pentatonic 1, Intervals Shown as A Minor

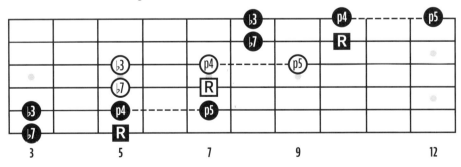

Diagonal Fingering 1 in the Five Main Guitar Keys

Use the diagrams below to help move the cell exercises to new keys.

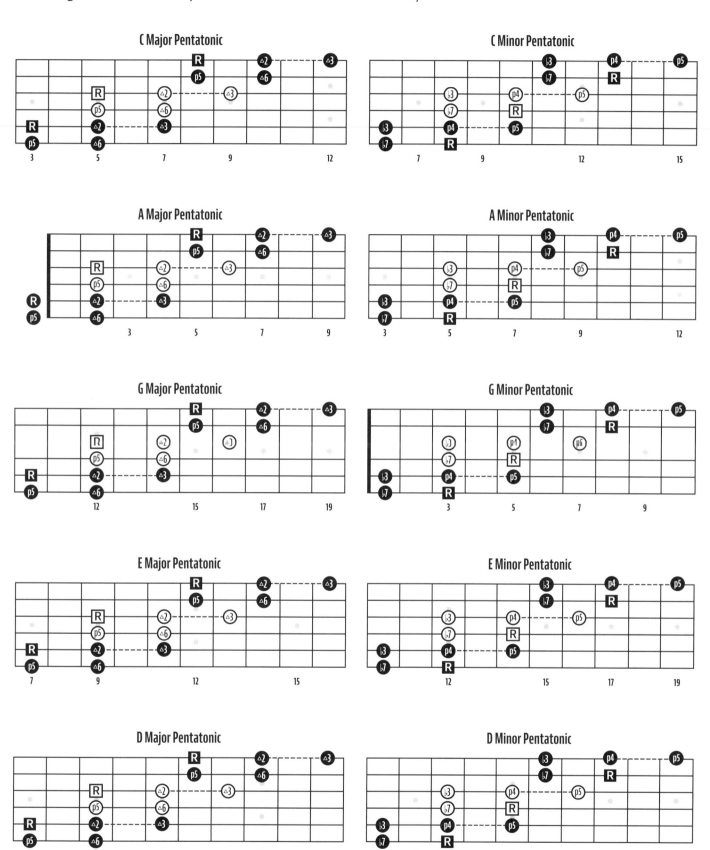

Descending Cells, Diagonal 1 Played on the Upper Strings

First play the following phrases as written, then apply a rhythm from below or from the Appendix. Use the phrase blueprints, scale diagrams, and corresponding audio tracks to change keys. Continue playing the rhythm and improvise your note choices using these backing tracks: C Major Backing Track 384 for Rhythm 1, G Blues Backing Track 400 for Rhythm 2, E Major Backing Track 385 for Rhythm 3, and E Blues Backing Track 401 for Rhythm 4.

Track 44 - Rhythm 1, Key of C

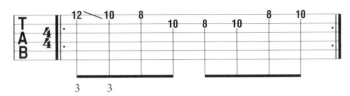
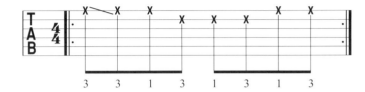

Track 45 - Rhythm 2, Key of G Minor

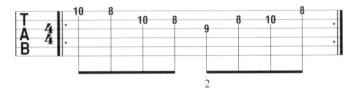
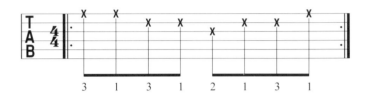

Track 46 - Rhythm 3, Key of E

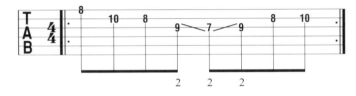
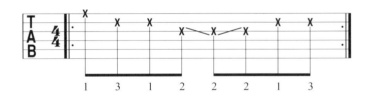

Track 47 - Rhythm 4, Key of E Minor

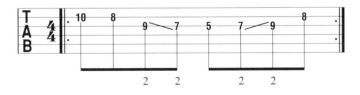
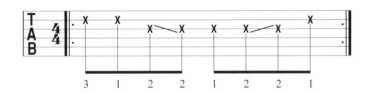

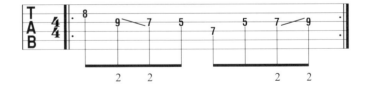
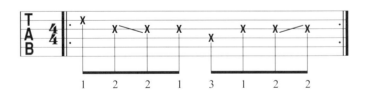

Ascending Cells, Diagonal 1 Played on the Upper Strings

First play the following phrases as written, then apply a rhythm from below or from the Appendix. Use the phrase blueprints, scale diagrams, and corresponding audio tracks to change keys. Continue playing the rhythm and improvise your note choices using these backing tracks: C Major Backing Track 384 for Rhythm 1, G Blues Backing Track 400 for Rhythm 2, E Major Backing Track 385 for Rhythm 3, and E Blues Backing Track 401 for Rhythm 4.

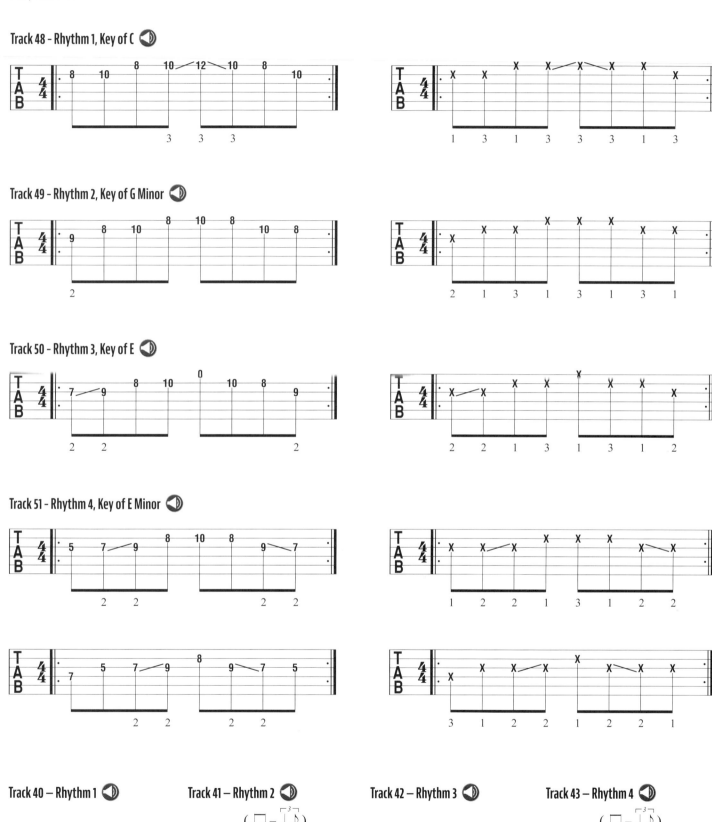

More Ideas for Improvising

Now that you've had some experience improvising with Pentatonic Fingering 1, let's explore using some of the same devices in new combinations with Diagonal Fingering 1. New ideas can be generated by putting the things you already know together in new ways. Remember that it's a good idea to repeat each measure separately to absorb the concept, then string them together to play the exercise. Apply these new combinations to step 3 of your cell practice.

Repeat a Note/Two-Note Combinations

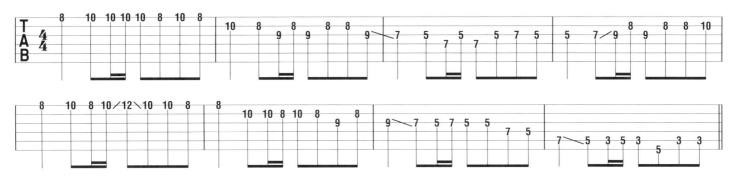

Repeat a Note/Three-Note Combinations

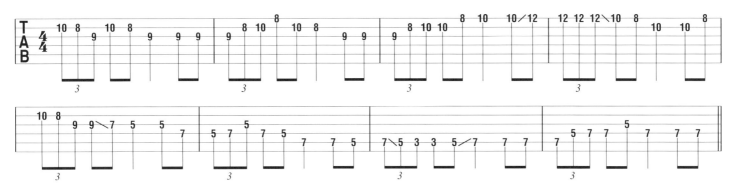

Two-Note/Three-Note Combinations

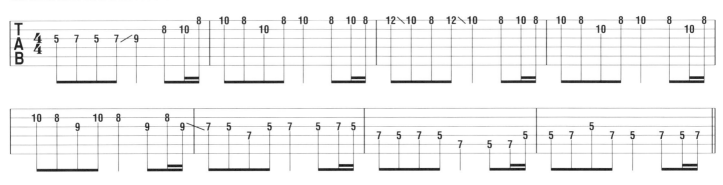

Repeat a Note/Two-Note/Three-Note Combinations

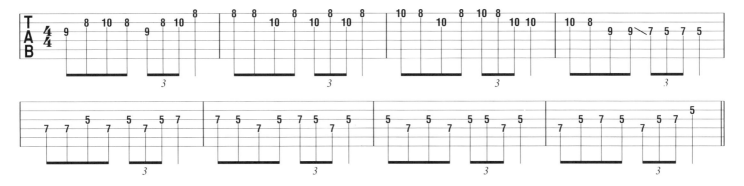

Descending Cells, Diagonal 1 Played on the Lower Strings

First play the following phrases as written, then apply a rhythm from below or from the Appendix. Use the phrase blueprints, scale diagrams, and corresponding audio tracks to change keys. Continue playing the rhythm and improvise your note choices using these backing tracks: C Major Backing Track 384 for Rhythm 1, G Blues Backing Track 400 for Rhythm 2, E Major Backing Track 385 for Rhythm 3, and E Blues Backing Track 401 for Rhythm 4.

Track 52 – Rhythm 1, Key of C

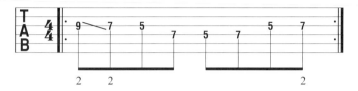 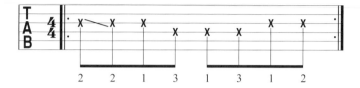

Track 53 – Rhythm 2, Key of G Minor

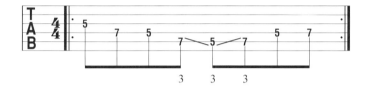 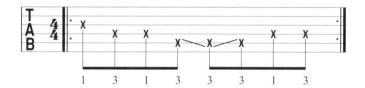

Track 54 – Rhythm 3, Key of E

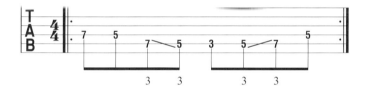 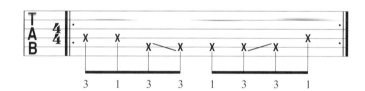

Track 55 – Rhythm 4, Key of E Minor

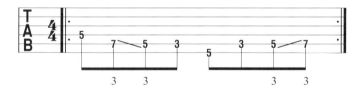 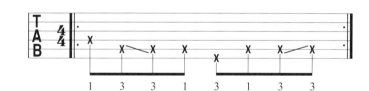

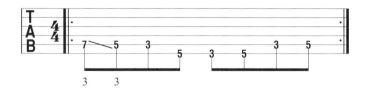 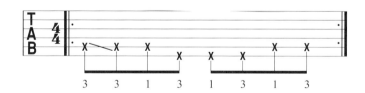

Track 40 – Rhythm 1   Track 41 – Rhythm 2   Track 42 – Rhythm 3   Track 43 – Rhythm 4

Ascending Cells, Diagonal 1 Played on the Lower Strings

First play the following phrases as written, then apply a rhythm from below or from the Appendix. Use the phrase blueprints, scale diagrams, and corresponding audio tracks to change keys. Continue playing the rhythm and improvise your note choices using these backing tracks: C Major Backing Track 384 for Rhythm 1, G Blues Backing Track 400 for Rhythm 2, E Major Backing Track 385 for Rhythm 3, and E Blues Backing Track 401 for Rhythm 4.

Track 56 - Rhythm 1, Key of C

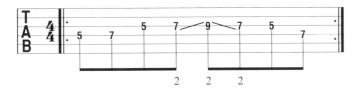
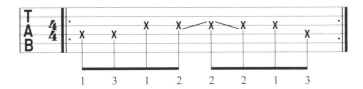

Track 57 - Rhythm 2, Key of G Minor

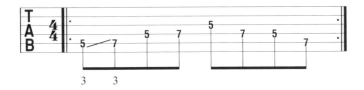
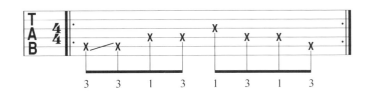

Track 58 - Rhythm 3, Key of E

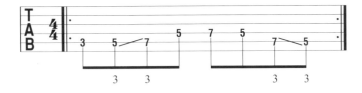
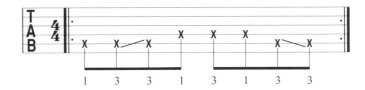

Track 59 - Rhythm 4, Key of E Minor

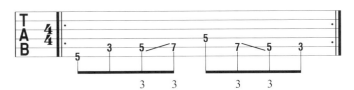
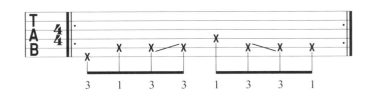

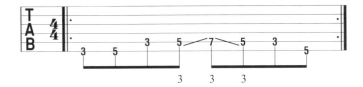
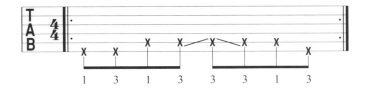

Track 40 – Rhythm 1   **Track 41 – Rhythm 2**   **Track 42 – Rhythm 3**   **Track 43 – Rhythm 4**

Ideas for Efficient Practice Sessions

As you progress through this book and start adding new material, it is a good idea to take stock of what you have learned already and formulate a game plan for future practice. The idea is to keep the older material fresh while adding the new material to your existing musical vocabulary. Start by practicing the newest material first while it is fresh and you are most likely to retain new information. Following is a new example of how you might approach a practice session.

- Pick a key for your session or change keys with each exercise. Keep track of which key your session is in so that you can play a different key in your next session.

- Start with a Diagonal 1 visualization exercise to get used to the pattern you are working with. Pay attention to the symmetry of the five-note groups.

- Play some Diagonal 1 cell exercises with rhythms and improvise. Try using one-, two-, and three-note patterns, then play freely within the scale.

- Go back to Fingering 1 and play and improvise with some cells.

- Try switching between Fingering 1 and Diagonal 1 while improvising, observing where the scales intersect with each other.

- Work on one of the written solo examples.

Of course there are many ways that you can organize the material, and the above are just some possibilities. The main thing is to stay focused throughout your practice session. Try to make it through several topics without spending the entire allotted time on only one of them.

To incorporate Fingering 1 and Diagonal 1, many solos begin in the one-position fingering and shift diagonally, higher or lower, as needed. Try the example below to get started.

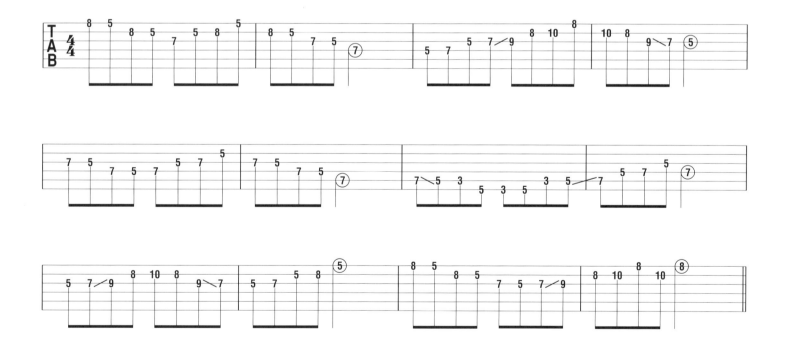

31

Descending Cells Connected

Track 60 – Rhythm 1, Key of C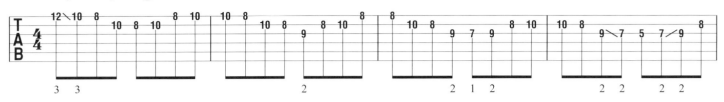

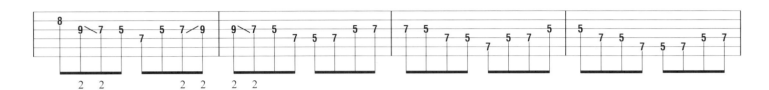

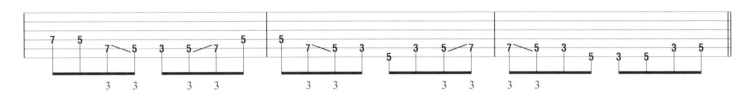

Descending Connected Blueprint

Track 61 – Rhythm 2, Key of G Minor 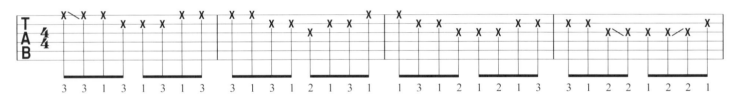   Track 62 – Rhythm 3, Key of E   Track 63 – Rhythm 4, Key of E Minor

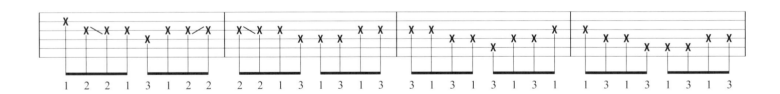

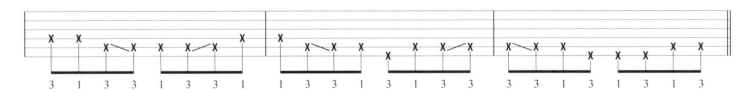

When you can play these easily, take the guide away and use: C Major Backing Track 384 for Rhythm 1, G Blues Backing Track 400 for Rhythm 2, E Major Backing Track 385 for Rhythm 3, and E Blues Backing Track 401 for Rhythm 4. More rhythms can be found in the Appendix.

Track 40 – Rhythm 1   Track 41 – Rhythm 2   Track 42 – Rhythm 3   Track 43 – Rhythm 4

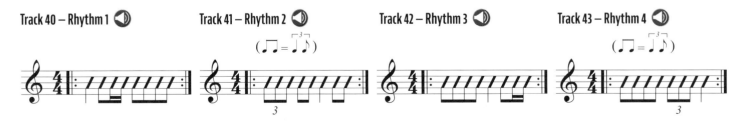

Ascending Cells Connected

Track 64 – Rhythm 1, Key of C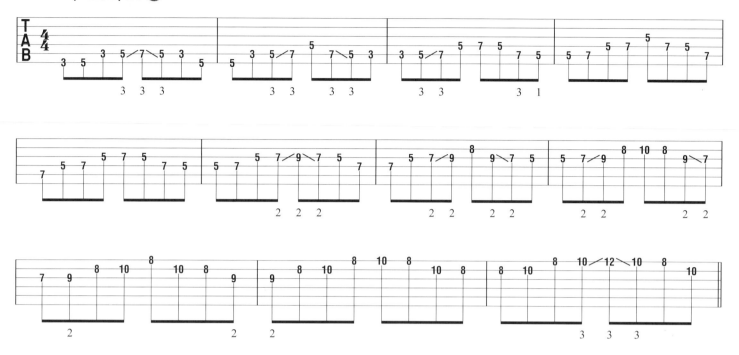

Ascending Connected Blueprint

Track 65 – Rhythm 2, Key of G Minor   Track 66 – Rhythm 3, Key of E   Track 67 – Rhythm 4, Key of E Minor

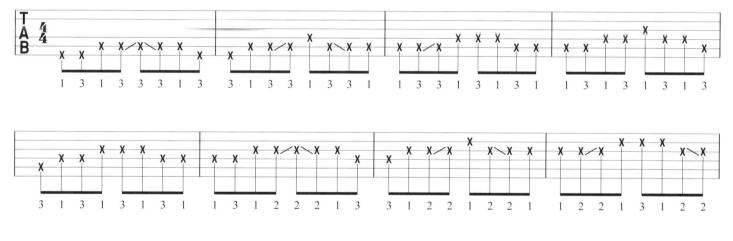

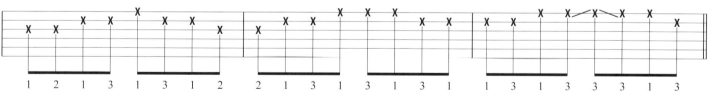

When you can play these easily, take the guide away and use: C Major Backing Track 384 for Rhythm 1, G Blues Backing Track 400 for Rhythm 2, E Major Backing Track 385 for Rhythm 3, and E Blues Backing Track 401 for Rhythm 4. More rhythms can be found in the Appendix.

Track 40 – Rhythm 1   Track 41 – Rhythm 2   Track 42 – Rhythm 3   Track 43 – Rhythm 4

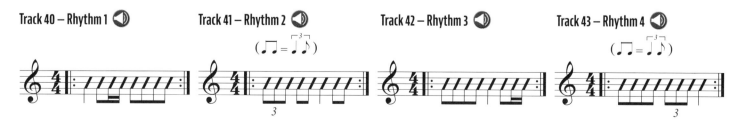

Solo 5: Two-Measure Phrases Using C Major Diagonal 1

Track 68 Backing Track 384

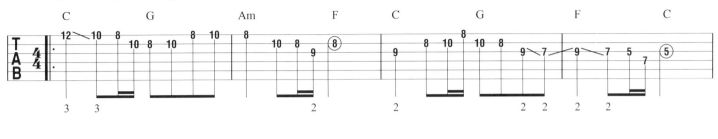

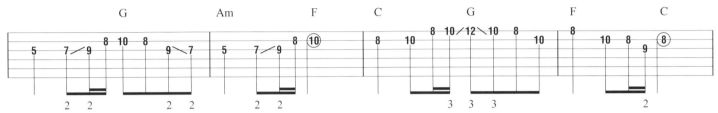

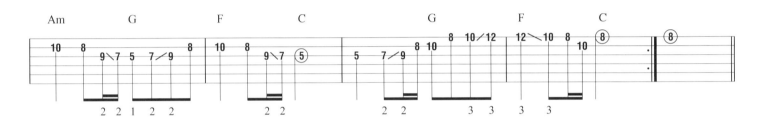

Solo 6: Two-Measure Phrases Using G Minor Diagonal 1

Track 69 Backing Track 400

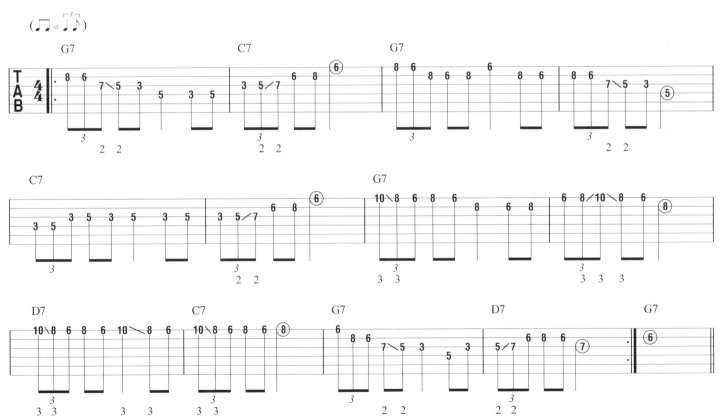

Solo 7: Two-Measure Phrases Using E Major Diagonal 1

Track 70  Backing Track 385

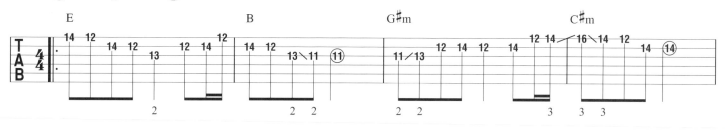

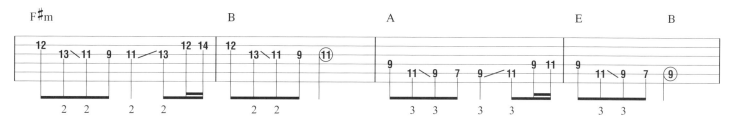

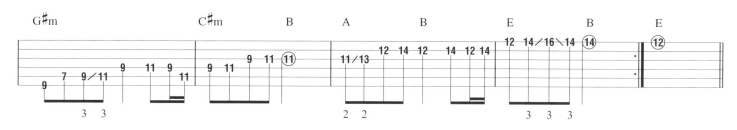

Solo 8: Two-Measure Phrases Using E Minor Diagonal 1

Track 71  Backing Track 401

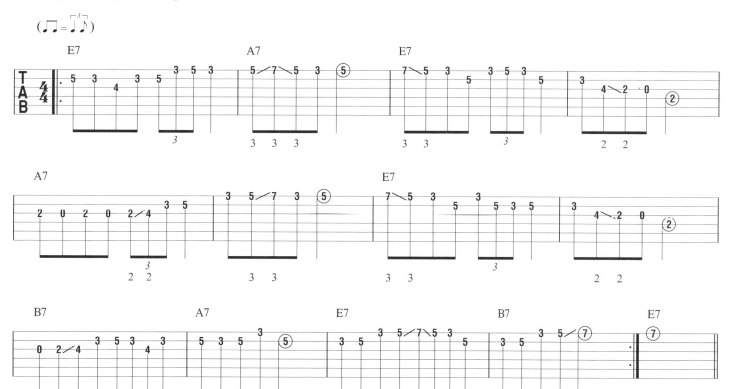

Chapter 3: Pentatonic Fingering 4

Just like Pentatonic Fingering 1, there are two main ways to finger this scale shape. The alternate fingering utilizes the strongest fingers, and you may find yourself switching between fingerings depending on the situation. Start by simply playing up and down the patterns to acquaint yourself with them.

Pentatonic Fingering 4

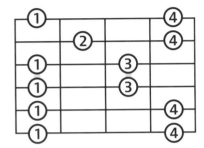

Alternate Fingering

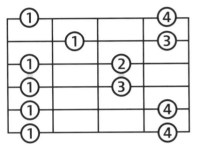

Once again, to find the major chord and scale sound, we will line the scale up with our fourth finger on the root. This time we will find the root on string 5. Play the exercise to hear the scale in a major context. If you have trouble playing the chord, try removing the fourth-finger note, but keep in mind its location for finding the scale.

G Chord Played with the Fourth Finger on the Fifth String
(Fifth-String-Root Open C Chord Shape)

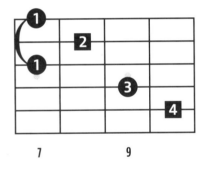

G Pentatonic Fingering 4
(Line Your Fourth Finger Up on the Root)

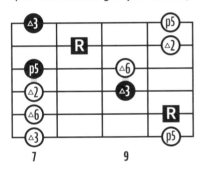

Notice where the notes of the chord are located within the scale.

Track 72

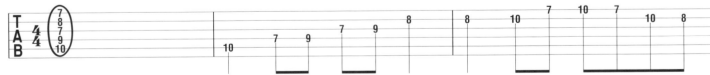

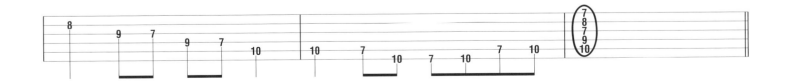

36

As with our Fingering 1 for the pentatonic scale, the second main usage of our scale is the minor sound obtained by lining up and starting the scale on your first finger. The root will also be located on string 5, and a key visualization is seeing the open Am shape within the fingering. Observe the sound and feel of the minor scale as you play the example below.

Em Chord Played with the First Finger on the Fifth String
(Fifth-String-Root Open Am Chord Shape)

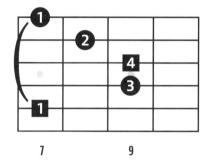

E Minor Pentatonic Fingering 4
(Line Your First Finger Up on the Root)

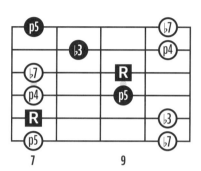

Notice where the notes of the chord are located within the scale.

Track 73

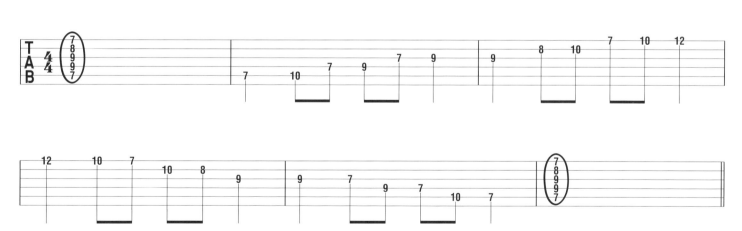

Pentatonic Fingering 4 in the Five Main Guitar Keys

Use the charts below to move the scale around the fretboard. Use the black dots to visualize the chord within the scale pattern.

C Major Pentatonic
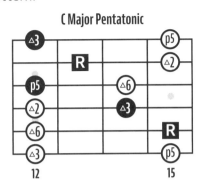

C Minor Pentatonic
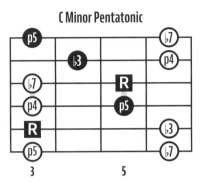

A Major Pentatonic
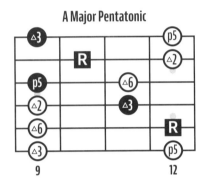

A Minor Pentatonic
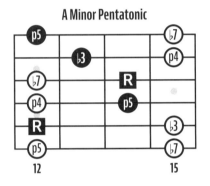

G Major Pentatonic
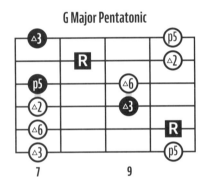

G Minor Pentatonic
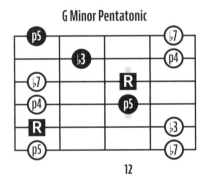

E Major Pentatonic
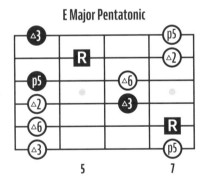

E Minor Pentatonic
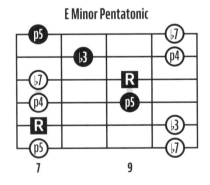

D Major Pentatonic
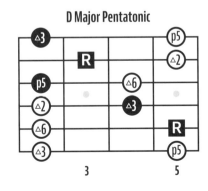

D Minor Pentatonic
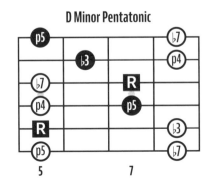

Descending Four-Note Cells Played on the Upper Strings

First play the following phrases as written, then apply a rhythm from below or from the Appendix. Use the phrase blueprints, scale diagrams, and corresponding audio tracks to change keys. Continue playing the rhythm and improvise your note choices using these backing tracks: G Major Backing Track 386 for Rhythm 1, D Blues Backing Track 402 for Rhythm 2, A Major Backing Track 387 for Rhythm 3, and C Blues Backing Track 399 for Rhythm 4.

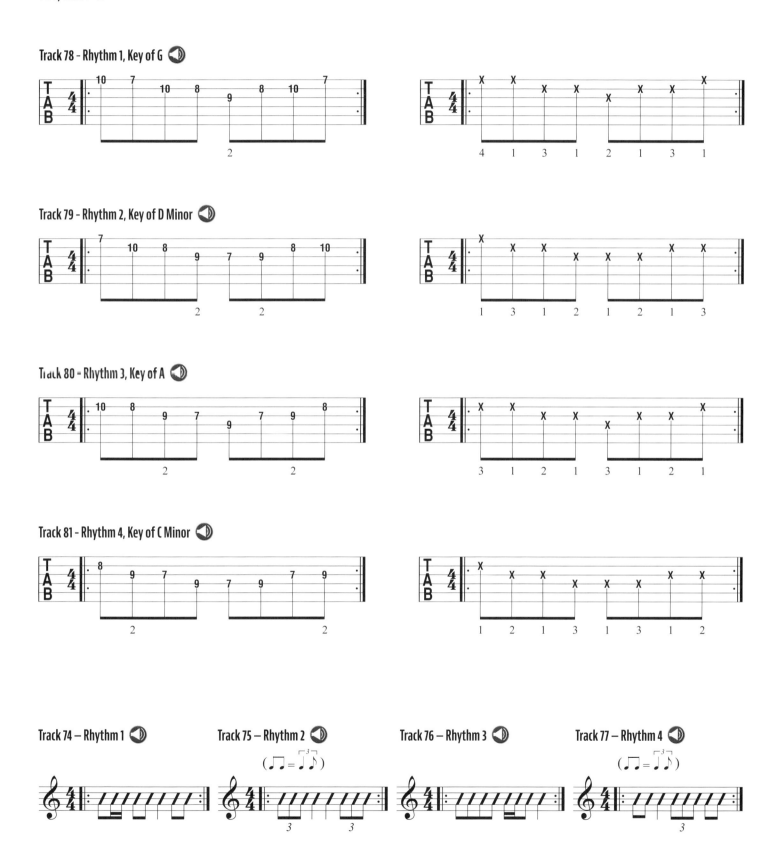

Track 78 - Rhythm 1, Key of G

Track 79 - Rhythm 2, Key of D Minor

Track 80 - Rhythm 3, Key of A

Track 81 - Rhythm 4, Key of C Minor

Track 74 – Rhythm 1   Track 75 – Rhythm 2   Track 76 – Rhythm 3   Track 77 – Rhythm 4

Ascending Four-Note Cells Played on the Upper Strings

First play the following phrases as written, then apply a rhythm from below or from the Appendix. Use the phrase blueprints, scale diagrams, and corresponding audio tracks to change keys. Continue playing the rhythm and improvise your note choices using these backing tracks: G Major Backing Track 386 for Rhythm 1, D Blues Backing Track 402 for Rhythm 2, A Major Backing Track 387 for Rhythm 3, and C Blues Backing Track 399 for Rhythm 4.

Track 82 – Rhythm 1, Key of G

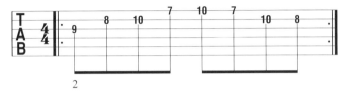 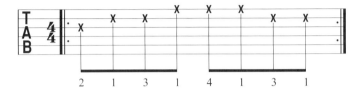

Track 83 – Rhythm 2, Key of D Minor

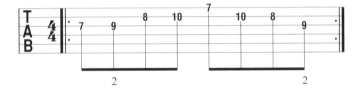 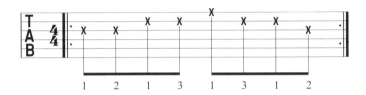

Track 84 – Rhythm 3, Key of A

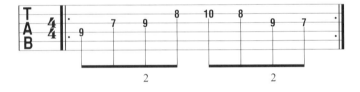 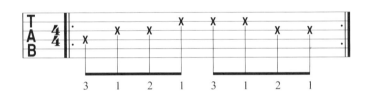

Track 85 – Rhythm 4, Key of C Minor

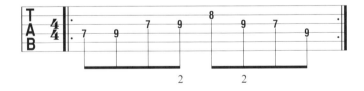 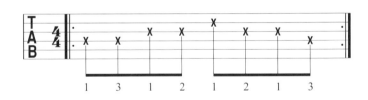

Track 74 – Rhythm 1 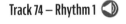 Track 75 – Rhythm 2  Track 76 – Rhythm 3  Track 77 – Rhythm 4

 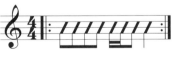 

More Ideas for Improvising

A great way to generate new patterns is to reorder the notes in a phrase. Doing so can provide a break from moving up and down a scale in a step-wise fashion. Let's examine the possibilities presented with a three-note phrase.

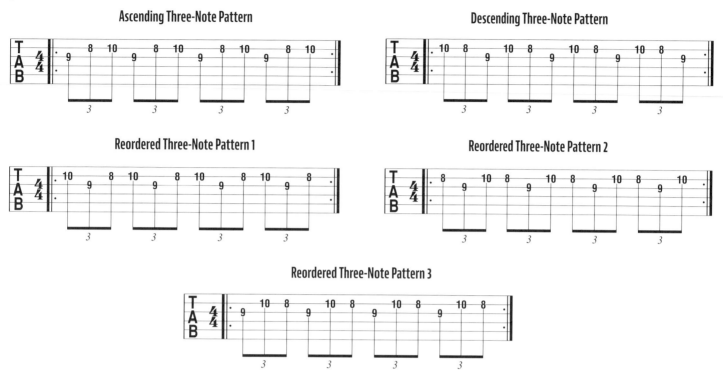

Ascending Three-Note Pattern

Descending Three-Note Pattern

Reordered Three-Note Pattern 1

Reordered Three-Note Pattern 2

Reordered Three-Note Pattern 3

The following examples use each of the above patterns in different combinations. Try playing each measure repeatedly then string them together. Make a conscious effort to practice improvising with these ideas as you practice the cell exercises.

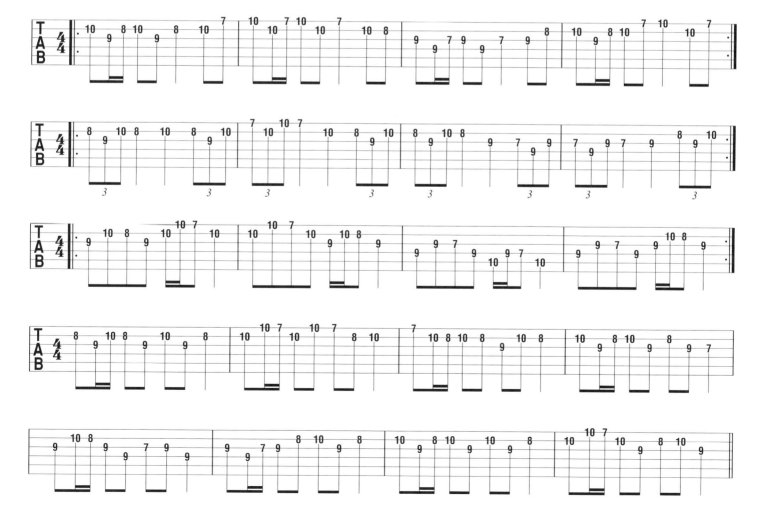

Descending Four-Note Cells Played on the Lower Strings

First play the following phrases as written, then apply a rhythm from below or from the Appendix. Use the phrase blueprints, scale diagrams, and corresponding audio tracks to change keys. Continue playing the rhythm and improvise your note choices using these backing tracks: G Major Backing Track 386 for Rhythm 1, D Blues Backing Track 402 for Rhythm 2, A Major Backing Track 387 for Rhythm 3, and C Blues Backing Track 399 for Rhythm 4.

Track 86 - Rhythm 1, Key of G

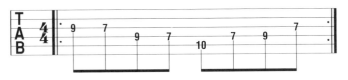 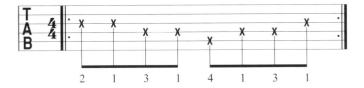

Track 87 - Rhythm 2, Key of D Minor

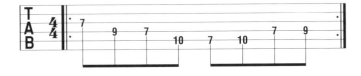 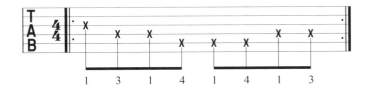

Track 88 - Rhythm 3, Key of A

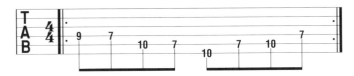 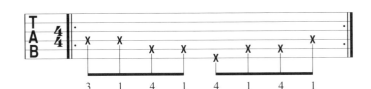

Track 89 - Rhythm 4, Key of C Minor

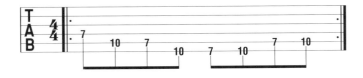 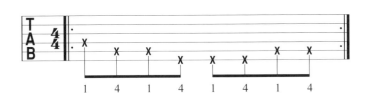

Track 74 – Rhythm 1   **Track 75 – Rhythm 2**   **Track 76 – Rhythm 3**   **Track 77 – Rhythm 4**

Ascending Four-Note Cells Played on the Lower Strings

First play the following phrases as written, then apply a rhythm from below or from the Appendix. Use the phrase blueprints, scale diagrams, and corresponding audio tracks to change keys. Continue playing the rhythm and improvise your note choices using these backing tracks: G Major Backing Track 386 for Rhythm 1, D Blues Backing Track 402 for Rhythm 2, A Major Backing Track 387 for Rhythm 3, and C Blues Backing Track 399 for Rhythm 4.

Track 90 - Rhythm 1, Key of G

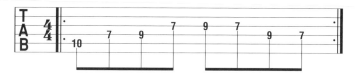 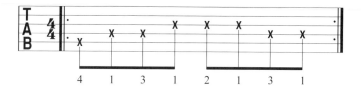

Track 91 - Rhythm 2, Key of D Minor

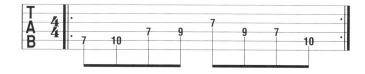 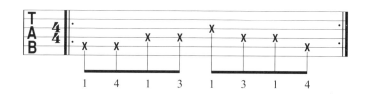

Track 92 - Rhythm 3, Key of A

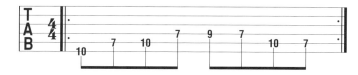 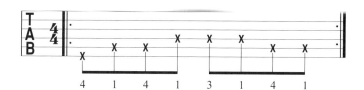

Track 93 - Rhythm 4, Key of C Minor

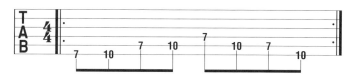 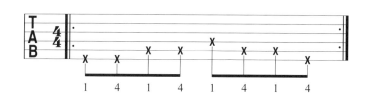

Track 74 – Rhythm 1   **Track 75 – Rhythm 2**   **Track 76 – Rhythm 3**   **Track 77 – Rhythm 4**

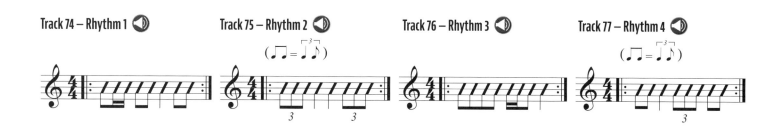

More Ideas for Practice Sessions

As we begin absorbing Fingering 4, it is a good idea to apply a similar practice plan to the ones we've used in Chapters 1 and 2. At first, you may need to spend more time on a single page, but in a relatively short amount of time, it is recommended to begin flipping pages and playing a cell or two from each of them. Let's look at an abbreviated version of the process.

1. Pick a cell from any chapter exercise and play it as written. Use the blueprint and diagrams in the chapter to relocate it to a new key.

2. Apply a rhythm pattern to the cell. After you've absorbed the rhythm, improvise with it for a few choruses with the backing track.

3. Turn the page! Grab another cell and rhythm pattern from any of the other ascending, descending, or connected exercise pages and repeat the process with a new rhythm. See how many different exercise pages you can tackle in a session!

4. Keep Fingering 1 and Diagonal 1 fresh by improvising with them. Try continuing a rhythm pattern from a Fingering 4 cell exercise into past fingerings.

5. Another great way to learn and incorporate Fingering 4 is to relocate phrases you've played in Fingering 1. In the following example, each phrase is relocated an octave higher in our new fingering. Apply rhythms from below as usual.

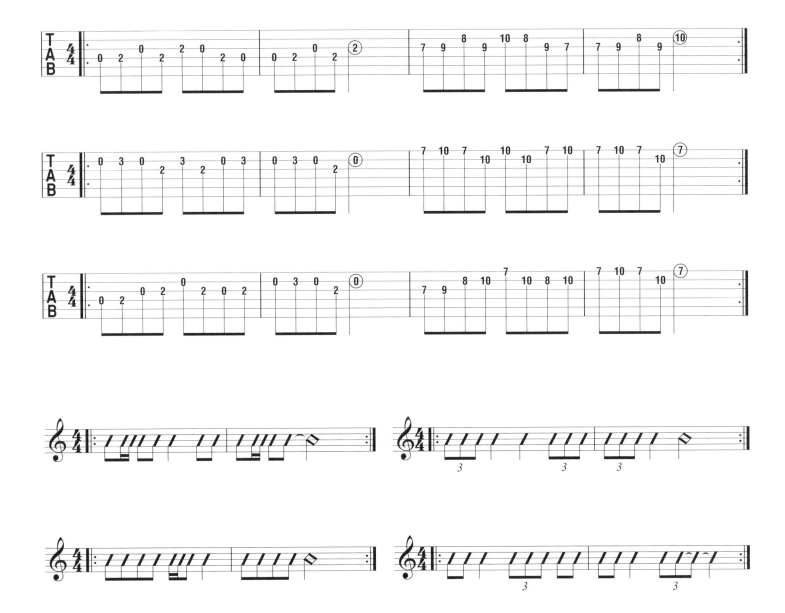

Descending Four-Note Cells Connected

Track 94 – Rhythm 1, Key of G

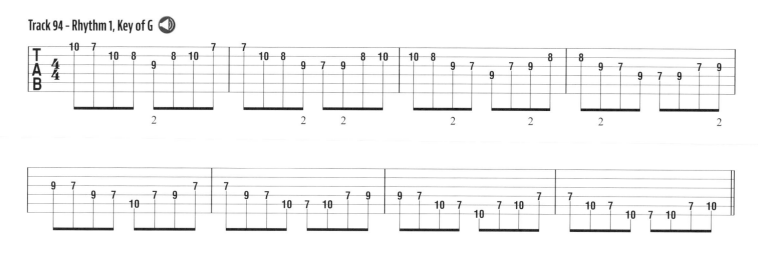

Descending Connected Blueprint

Track 95 – Rhythm 2, Key of D Minor   Track 96 – Rhythm 3, Key of A   Track 97 – Rhythm 4, Key of C Minor

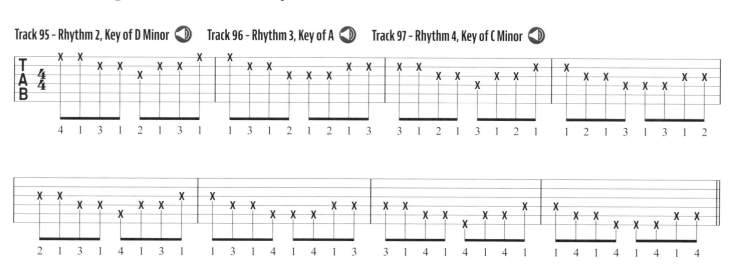

When you can play these easily, take the guide away and use: G Major Backing Track 386 for Rhythm 1, D Blues Backing Track 402 for Rhythm 2, A Major Backing Track 387 for Rhythm 3, and C Blues Backing Track 399 for Rhythm 4. More rhythms can be found in the Appendix.

Track 74 – Rhythm 1   Track 75 – Rhythm 2   Track 76 – Rhythm 3   Track 77 – Rhythm 4

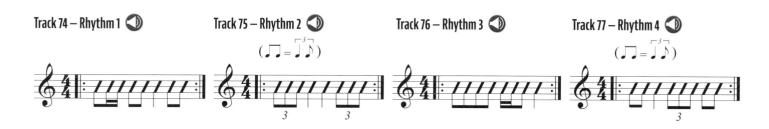

Ascending Four-Note Cells Connected

Track 98 – Rhythm 1, Key of G

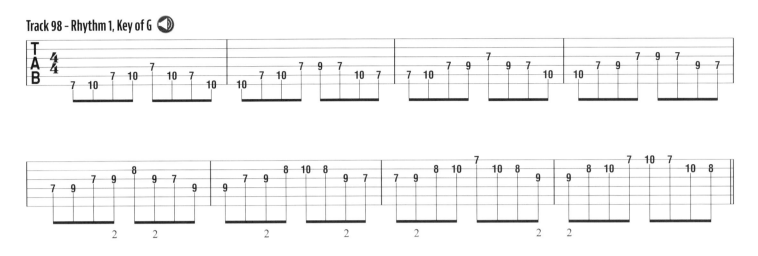

Ascending Connected Blueprint

Track 99 – Rhythm 2, Key of D Minor   Track 100 – Rhythm 3, Key of A   Track 101 – Rhythm 4, Key of C Minor

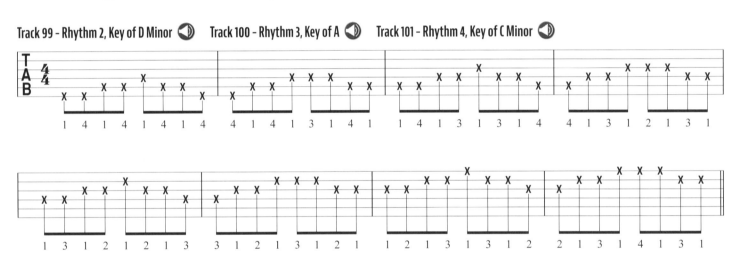

When you can play these easily, take the guide away and use: G Major Backing Track 386 for Rhythm 1, D Blues Backing Track 402 for Rhythm 2, A Major Backing Track 387 for Rhythm 3, and C Blues Backing Track 399 for Rhythm 4. More rhythms can be found in the Appendix.

Track 74 — Rhythm 1   Track 75 — Rhythm 2   Track 76 — Rhythm 3   Track 77 — Rhythm 4

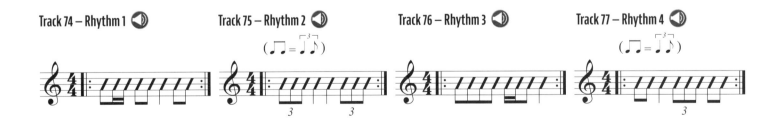

Solo 9: Two-Measure Phrases Using G Major Fingering 4

Track 102 🔊   Backing Track 386 🔊

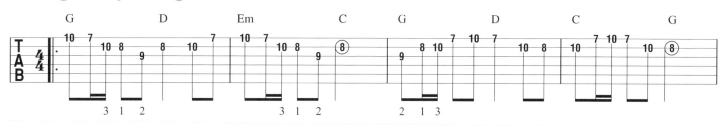

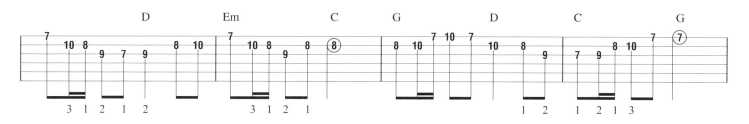

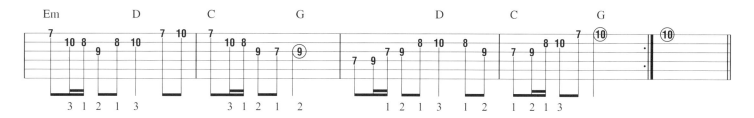

Solo 10: Two-Measure Phrases Using D Minor Fingering 4

Track 103 🔊   Backing Track 402 🔊

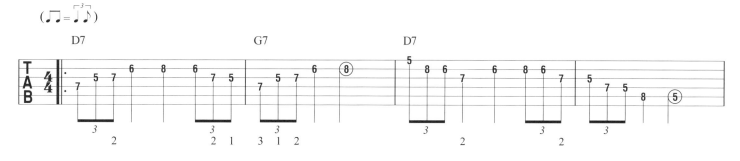

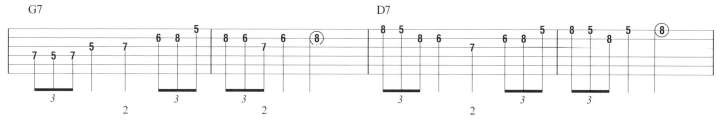

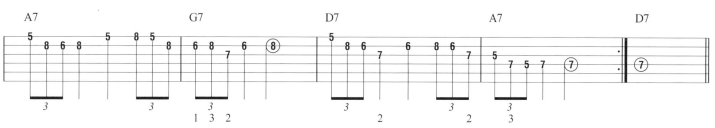

Solo 11: Two-Measure Phrases Using A Major Fingering 4

Track 104 🔊   Backing Track 387 🔊

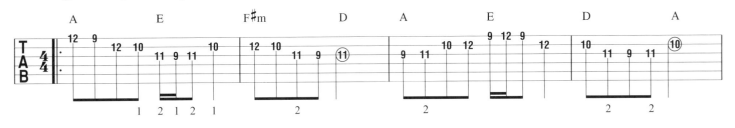

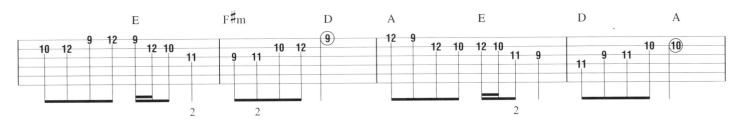

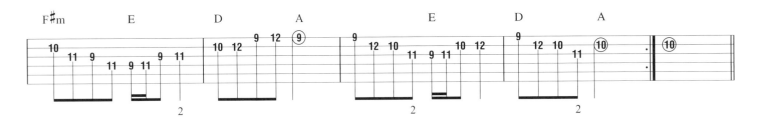

Solo 12: Two-Measure Phrases Using C Minor Fingering 4

Track 105 🔊   Backing Track 399 🔊

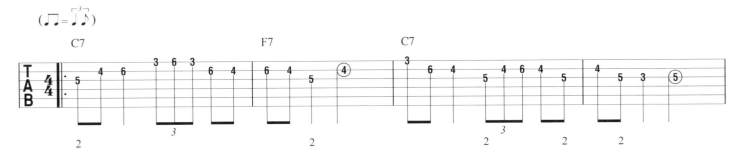

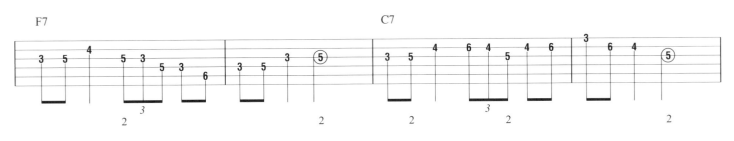

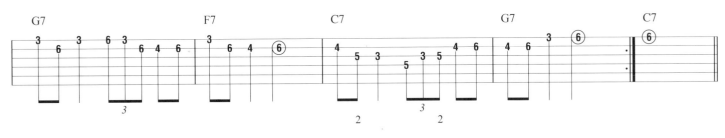

Chapter 4: Diagonal Pentatonic 4

Similar to Fingering 1, Diagonal Pentatonic 4 is a pattern that shifts through three pentatonic positions and lays diagonally along the fretboard. There are many approaches to using the diagonal patterns. You might start soloing in a one-position fingering and slide in and out of it as needed, or use the diagonal pattern to travel along the neck into a one-position fingering. As you explore the new diagonal fingering, observe the black dots and take note of where it intersects with Fingering 4.

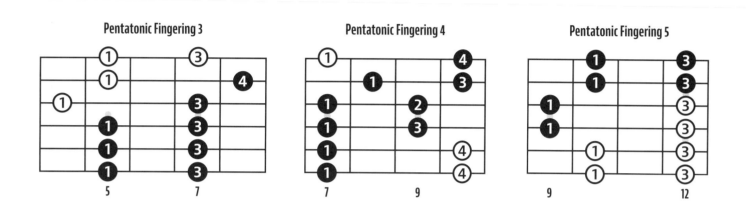

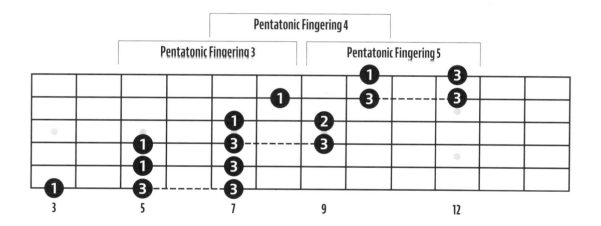

Visualizing Diagonal Pentatonic 4

Like our previous shifting pentatonic pattern, Diagonal Pentatonic 4 has three symmetrical groups of five notes. The difference is that they are upside down when compared to Diagonal Pentatonic 1, with three notes on the lower string and two on the upper string of each grouping. The white note markers help make each grouping stand out. Play the following exercises while studying the diagrams. Take special care to use your second finger where indicated.

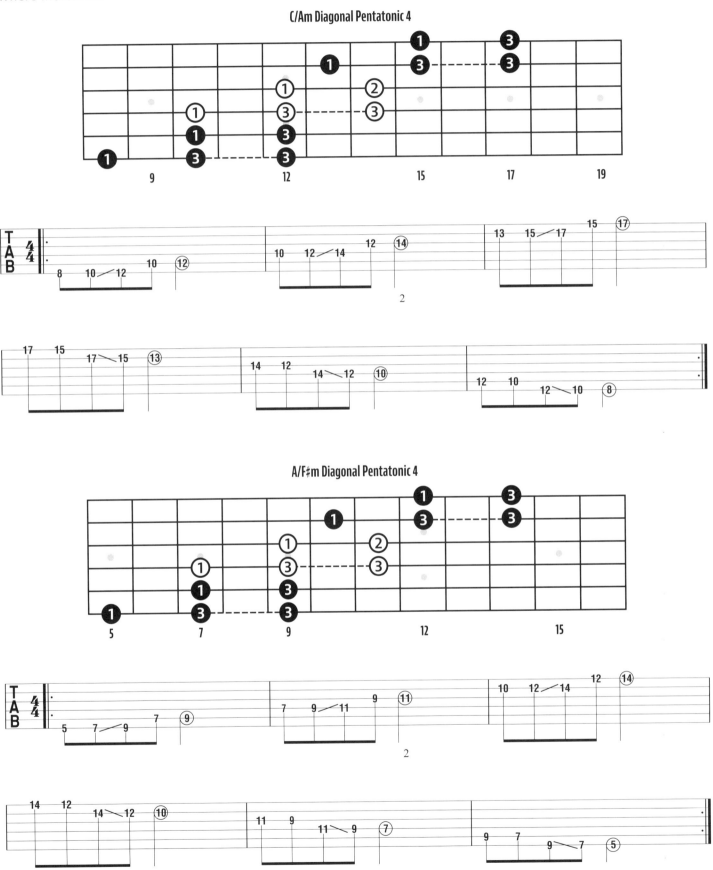

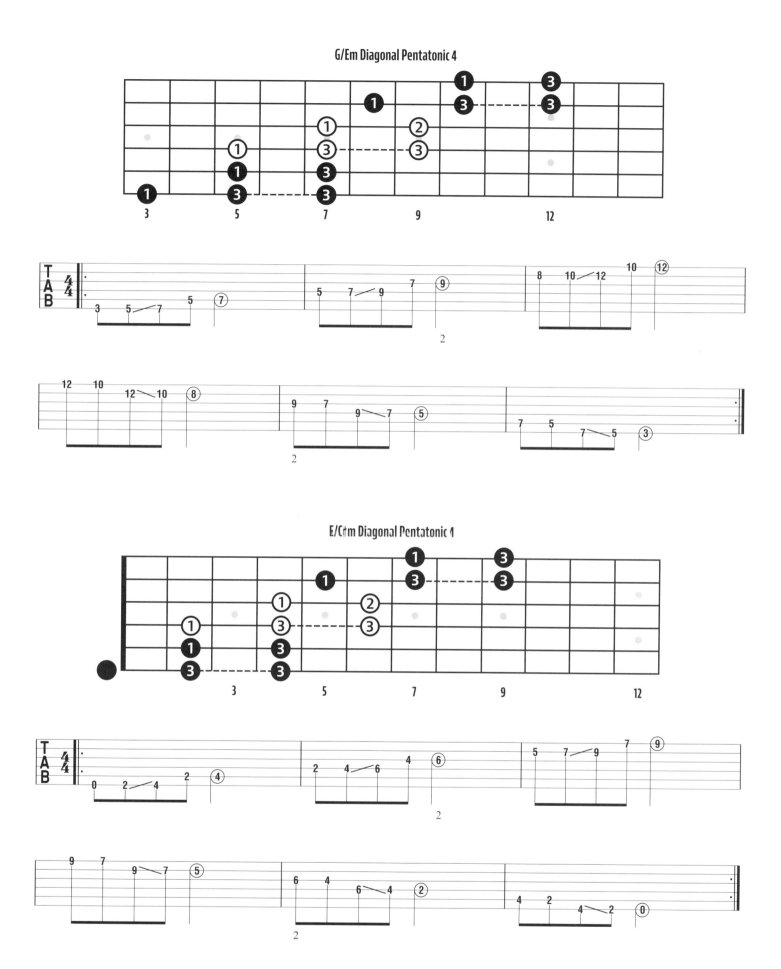

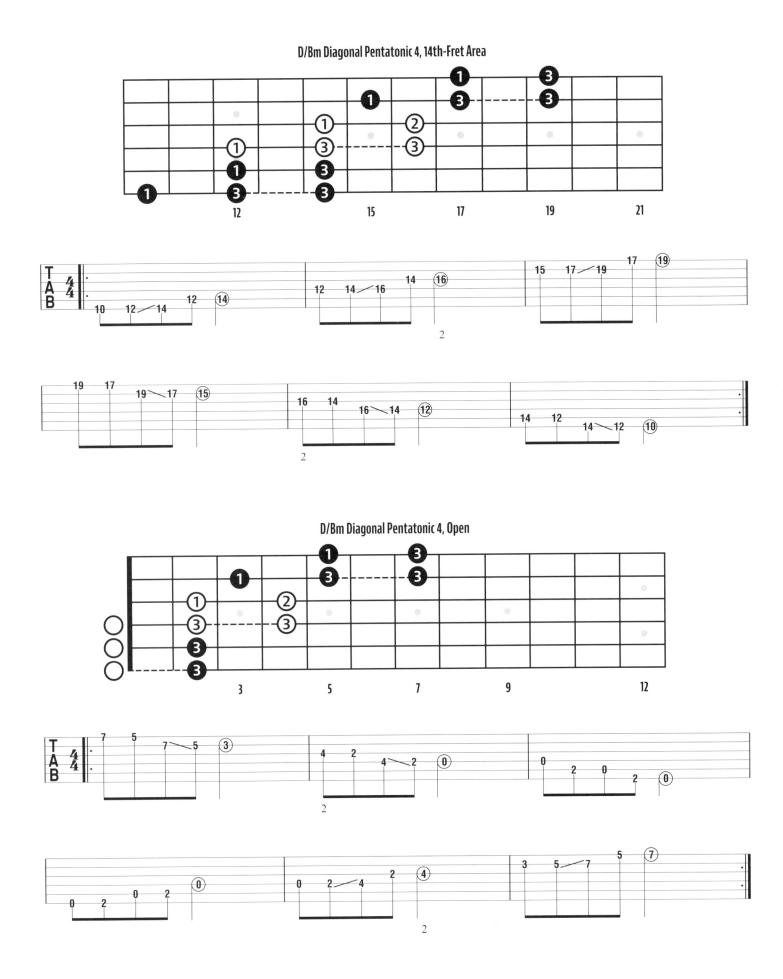

Diagonal Pentatonic Fingering 4

The diagrams below illustrate where our new fingering intersects with Pentatonic Fingering 4.

Pentatonic Fingering 4, Fifth-String Roots

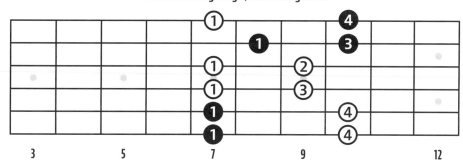

Diagonal Pentatonic 4, Travels Through Fingering 4

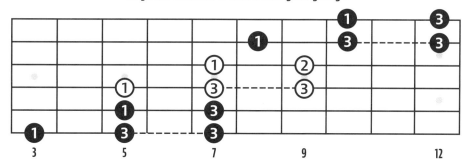

Diagonal Pentatonic 4 in G Major

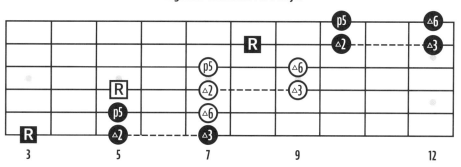

Diagonal Pentatonic 4 in E Minor

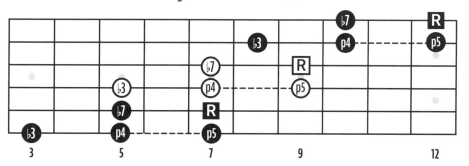

Diagonal Fingering 4 in the Five Main Guitar Keys

Use the diagrams below to help move the cell exercises to new keys.

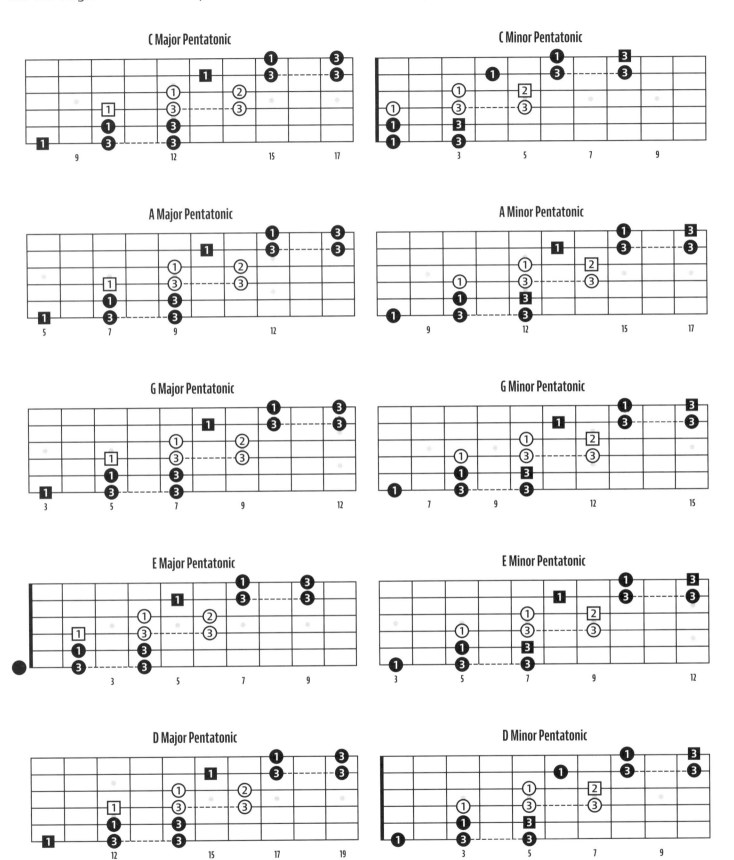

Descending Four-Note Cells Played on the Upper Strings

First play the following phrases as written, then apply a rhythm from below or from the Appendix. Use the phrase blueprints, scale diagrams, and corresponding audio tracks to change keys. Continue playing the rhythm and improvise your note choices using these backing tracks: G Major Backing Track 386 for Rhythm 1, D Blues Backing Track 402 for Rhythm 2, D Major Backing Track 388 for Rhythm 3, and E Blues Backing Track 401 for Rhythm 4.

Track 110 - Rhythm 1, Key of G

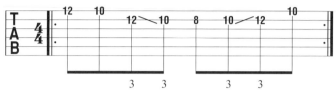 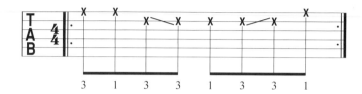

Track 111 - Rhythm 2, Key of D Minor

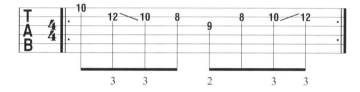 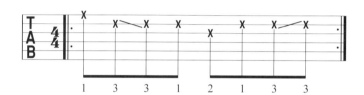

Track 112 - Rhythm 3, Key of D

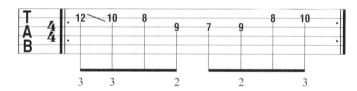 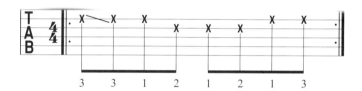

Track 113 - Rhythm 4, Key of E Minor

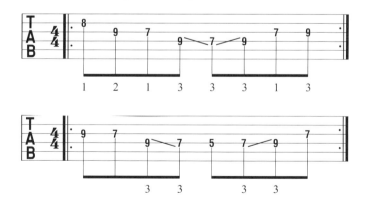 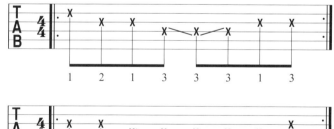

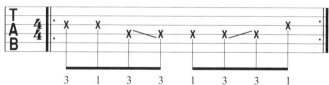

Track 106 — Rhythm 1 **Track 107 — Rhythm 2** **Track 108 — Rhythm 3** **Track 109 — Rhythm 4**

Ascending Four-Note Cells Played on the Upper Strings

First play the following phrases as written then apply a rhythm from below or from the Appendix. Use the phrase blueprints, scale diagrams, and corresponding audio tracks to change keys. Continue playing the rhythm and improvise your note choices using these backing tracks: G Major Backing Track 386 for Rhythm 1, D Blues Backing Track 402 for Rhythm 2, D Major Backing Track 388 for Rhythm 3, and E Blues Backing Track 401 for Rhythm 4.

Track 114 - Rhythm 1, Key of G

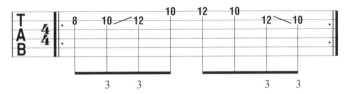
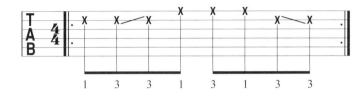

Track 115 - Rhythm 2, Key of D Minor

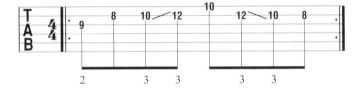
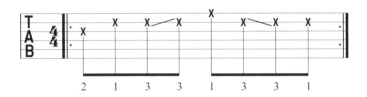

Track 116 - Rhythm 3, Key of D

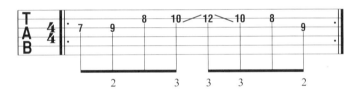
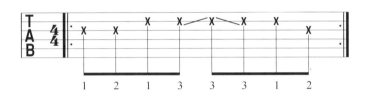

Track 117 - Rhythm 4, Key of E Minor

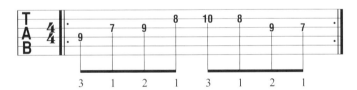
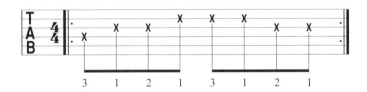

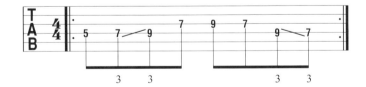
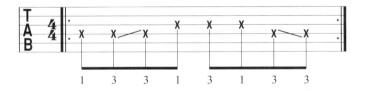

Track 106 – Rhythm 1   Track 107 – Rhythm 2   Track 108 – Rhythm 3   Track 109 – Rhythm 4

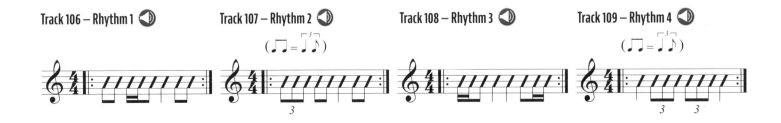

More Ideas for Improvising

Another device you can utilize to break up stepwise movement and add flair to your solos is to skip a note and move across adjacent strings. The following four patterns illustrate this idea. Try rolling your finger from string to string rather than picking up your entire finger and setting it back down on the next note. This will greatly increase your speed and efficiency.

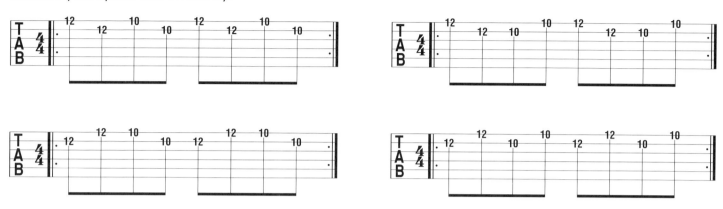

The following example places our new device next to others you've already improvised with.

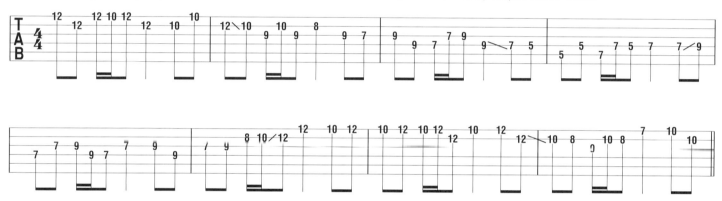

To take this concept even further, let's try skipping an entire string. These patterns create wider intervals and produce a unique sound. Use the same finger rolling method from above when necessary.

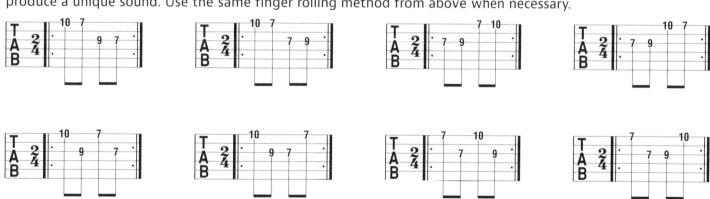

Remember to play each measure repeatedly, then string them together. Doing so allows you to absorb the phrases rather than just reading through the exercise. You can also try switching the rhythm back to straight eighth notes before attempting the phrase and rhythm together. Make a conscious effort to improvise with these concepts while practicing cell exercises.

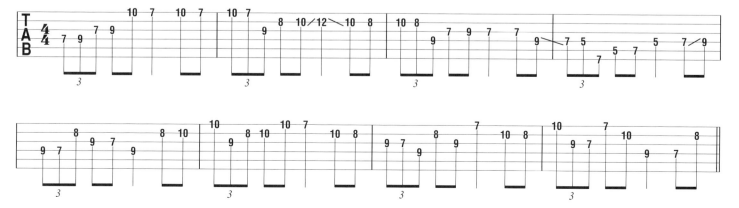

Descending Four-Note Cells Played on the Lower Strings

First play the following phrases as written, then apply a rhythm from below or from the Appendix. Use the phrase blueprints, scale diagrams, and corresponding audio tracks to change keys. Continue playing the rhythm and improvise your note choices using these backing tracks: G Major Backing Track 386 for Rhythm 1, D Blues Backing Track 402 for Rhythm 2, D Major Backing Track 388 for Rhythm 3, and E Blues Backing Track 401 for Rhythm 4.

Track 118 – Rhythm 1, Key of G

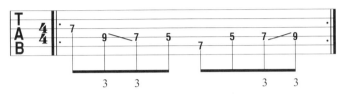
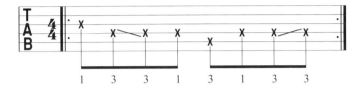

Track 119 – Rhythm 2, Key of D Minor

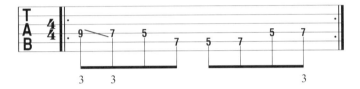
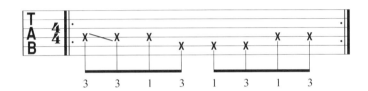

Track 120 – Rhythm 3, Key of D

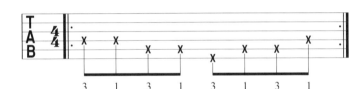

Track 121 – Rhythm 4, Key of E Minor

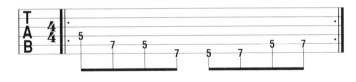
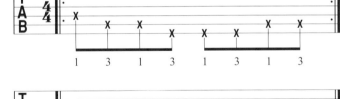

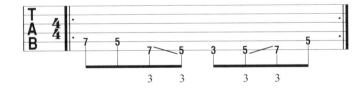
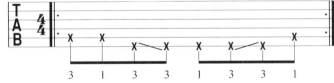

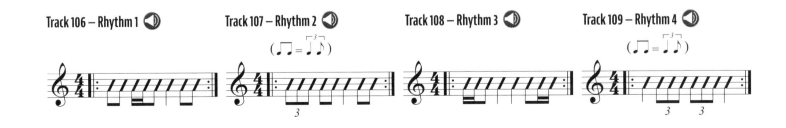

Track 106 – Rhythm 1   Track 107 – Rhythm 2   Track 108 – Rhythm 3   Track 109 – Rhythm 4

Ascending Four-Note Cells Played on the Lower Strings

First play the following phrases as written, then apply a rhythm from below or from the Appendix. Use the phrase blueprints, scale diagrams, and corresponding audio tracks to change keys. Continue playing the rhythm and improvise your note choices using these backing tracks: G Major Backing Track 386 for Rhythm 1, D Blues Backing Track 402 for Rhythm 2, D Major Backing Track 388 for Rhythm 3, and E Blues Backing Track 401 for Rhythm 4.

Track 122 - Rhythm 1, Key of G

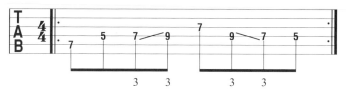 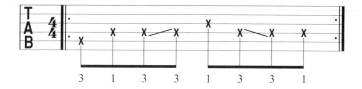

Track 123 - Rhythm 2, Key of D Minor

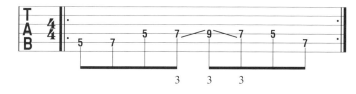 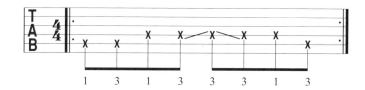

Track 124 - Rhythm 3, Key of D

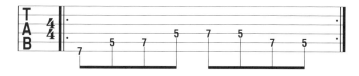 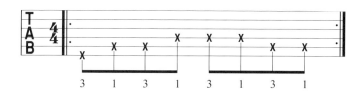

Track 125 - Rhythm 4, Key of E Minor

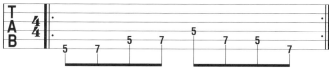 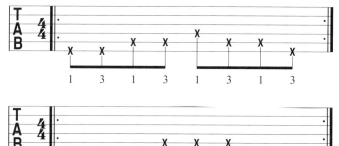

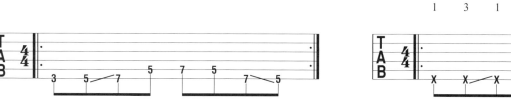

Track 106 – Rhythm 1    **Track 107 – Rhythm 2**    **Track 108 – Rhythm 3**    **Track 109 – Rhythm 4**

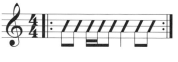  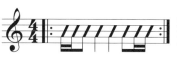

More Practice Ideas

Congratulations on making it to our final pentatonic fingering! Let's explore two concepts we worked on earlier to incorporate Diagonal Fingering 4 into our scale vocabulary. In the first example, we will mix Fingering 1 ideas with sliding into Diagonal Fingering 4 when we want to go higher or lower. Apply rhythms from the bottom of this page.

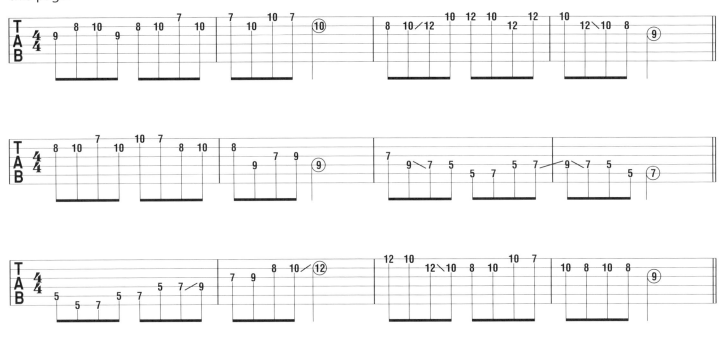

The next three exercises demonstrate how to move a phrase from Diagonal Fingering 1 to Diagonal Fingering 4. Developing this idea will enable you to carry a theme from one fingering to another, and repurpose your phrase vocabulary. Mix and match rhythms to make them come alive.

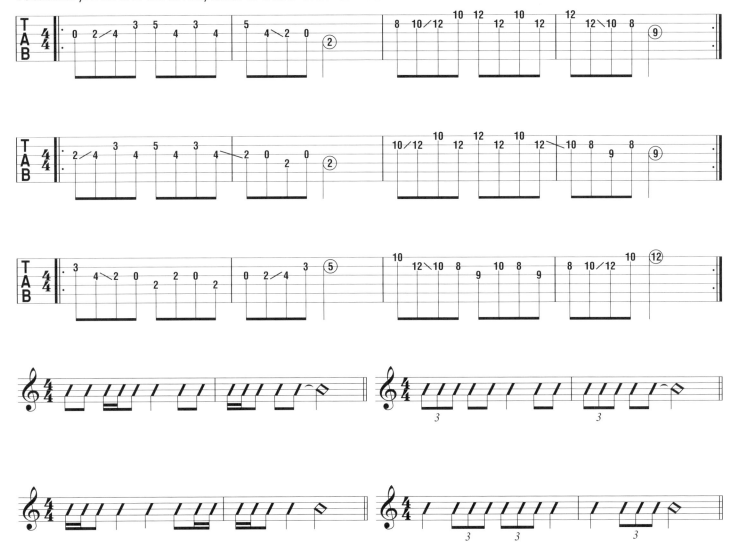

Descending Four-Note Cells Connected

Track 126 - Rhythm 1, Key of G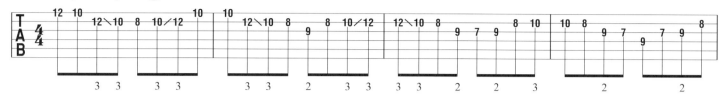

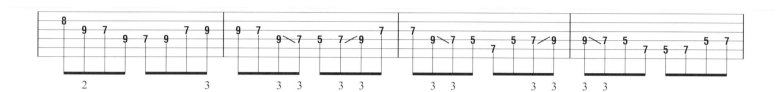

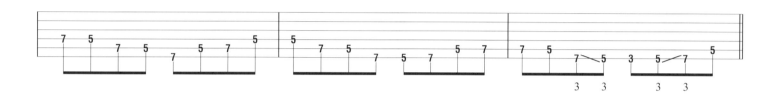

Descending Connected Blueprint

Track 127 - Rhythm 2, Key of D Minor   Track 128 - Rhythm 3, Key of D   Track 129 - Rhythm 4, Key of E Minor

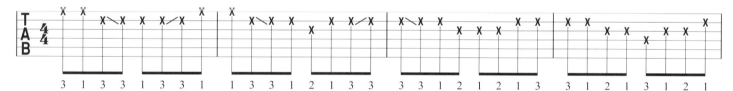

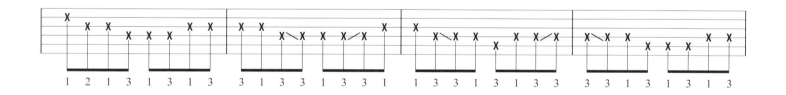

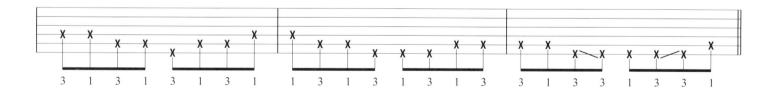

When you can play these easily, take the guide away and use: G Major Backing Track 386 for Rhythm 1, D Blues Backing Track 402 for Rhythm 2, D Major Backing Track 388 for Rhythm 3, and E Blues Backing Track 401 for Rhythm 4. More rhythms can be found in the Appendix.

Track 106 – Rhythm 1   Track 107 – Rhythm 2   Track 108 – Rhythm 3   Track 109 – Rhythm 4

Ascending Four-Note Cells Connected

Track 130 - Rhythm 1, Key of G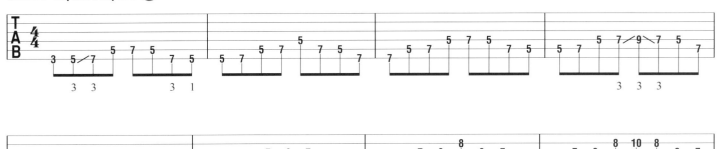

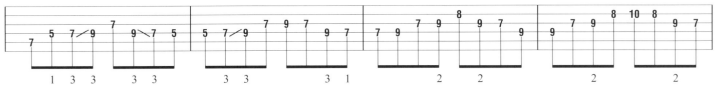

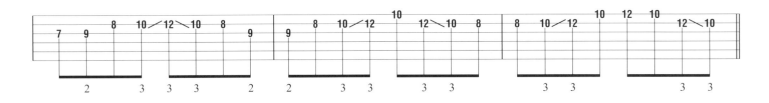

Ascending Connected Blueprint

Track 131 – Rhythm 2, Key of D Minor Track 132 – Rhythm 3, Key of D Track 133 – Rhythm 4, Key of E Minor

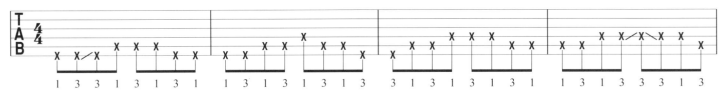

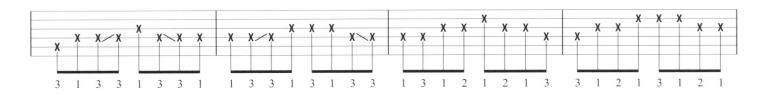

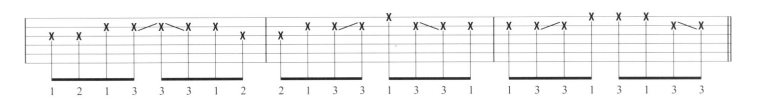

When you can play these easily, take the guide away and use: G Major Backing Track 386 for Rhythm 1, D Blues Backing Track 402 for Rhythm 2, D Major Backing Track 388 for Rhythm 3, and E Blues Backing Track 401 for Rhythm 4. More rhythms can be found in the Appendix.

Track 106 – Rhythm 1   Track 107 – Rhythm 2   Track 108 – Rhythm 3   Track 109 – Rhythm 4

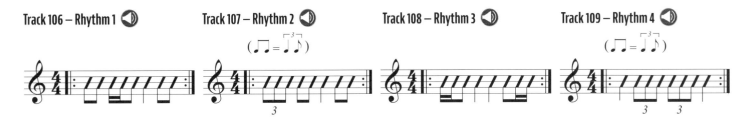

Solo 13: Two-Measure Phrases Using G Major Diagonal 4

Track 134 🔊   Backing Track 386 🔊

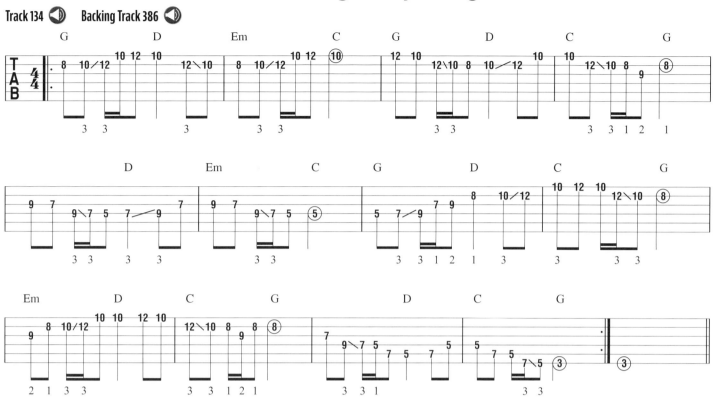

Solo 14: Two-Measure Phrases Using D Minor Diagonal 4

Track 135 🔊   Backing Track 402 🔊

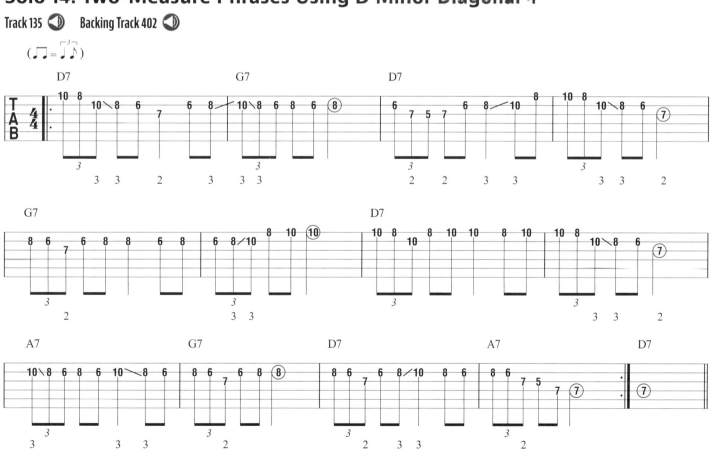

Solo 15: Two-Measure Phrases Using D Major Diagonal 4

Track 136 🔊   Backing Track 388 🔊

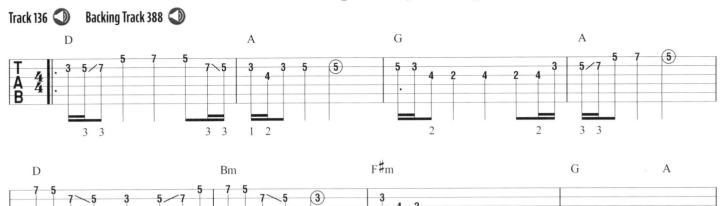

Solo 16: Two-Measure Phrases Using E Minor Diagonal 4

Track 137 🔊   Backing Track 401 🔊

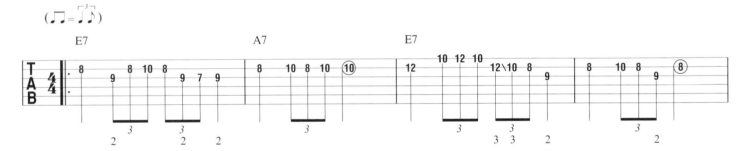

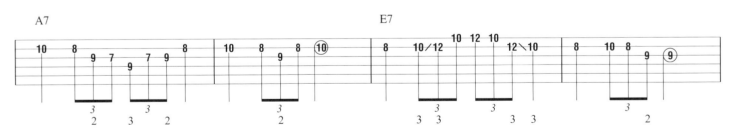

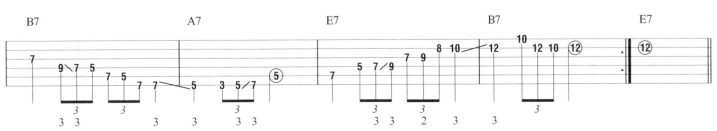

Chapter 5: Connecting the Fingerings

Now that you have learned Fingerings 1 and 4, and the diagonal patterns that correspond with them, our new challenge is to see each area on the fretboard and develop the ability to connect them while improvising. While it is possible to shift positions on any string, a great way to begin finding the next position is to use the lowest and highest note of each diagonal pattern. This idea can be summed up with the following sentence.

The lowest and highest note of each diagonal fingering is the connecting point to the next position.

In the following scale diagrams, the black dots show Fingering 1 and white dots show Fingering 4. The triangles indicate notes both fingerings have in common. Double triangles indicate the lowest or highest note of each position. *When you reach a double triangle, make a three-fret shift to get into the next position.* Begin with the key of C, playing each exercise as written.

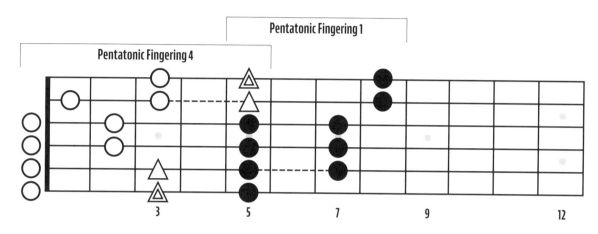

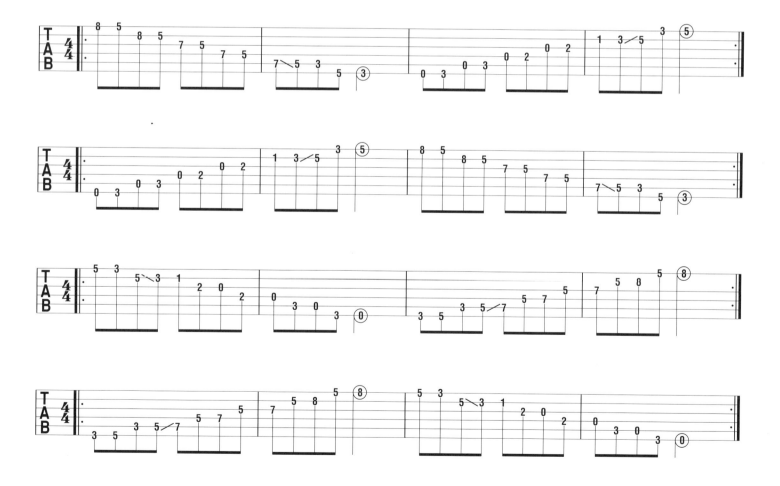

C/Am from the 5th to 15th Fret

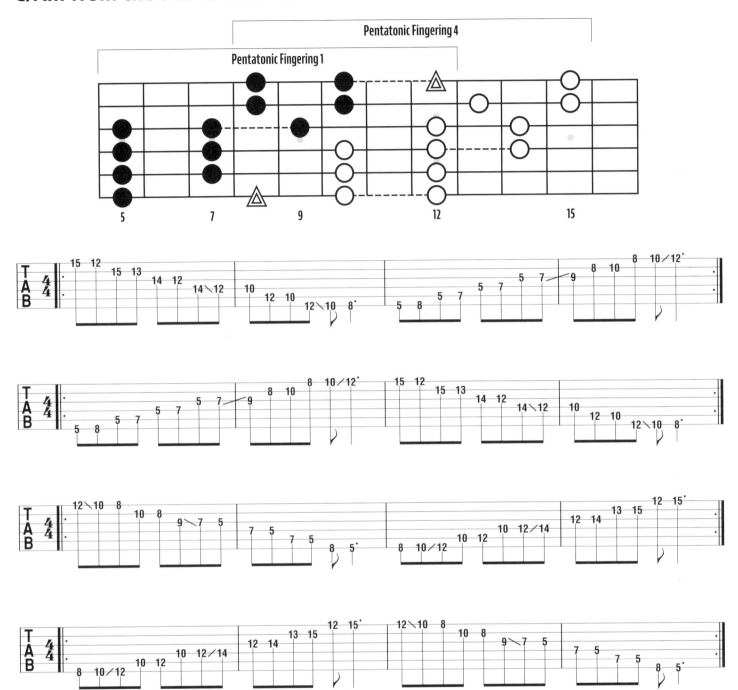

When you feel ready, try applying a rhythm from below to make these examples musical. Note that the patterns are two measures long to fit each phrase. Use any C, A Minor, or A Blues Backing Tracks to play the examples over.

Track 138

Track 139

More Rhythms

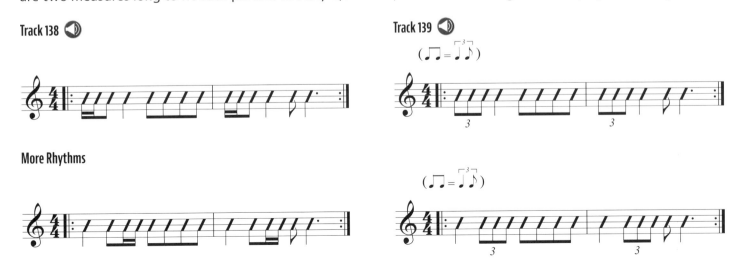

66

C/Am from the 12th to 20th Fret

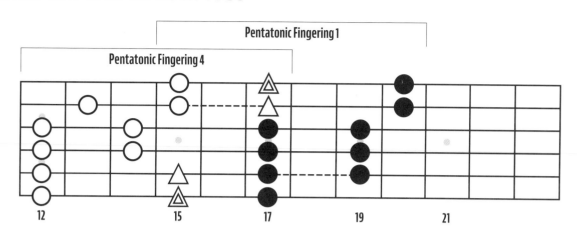

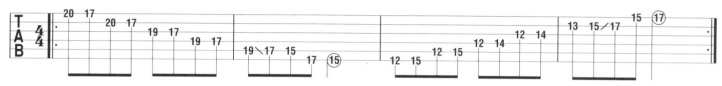

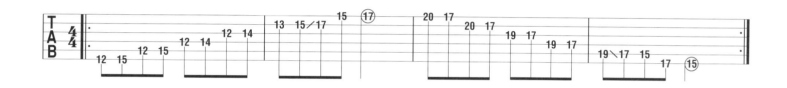

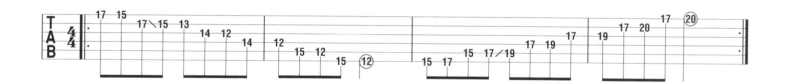

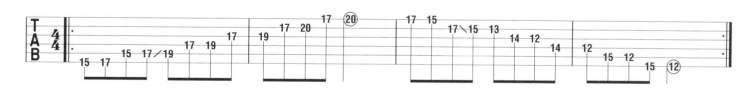

Use any C, A Minor, or A Blues Backing Tracks to play the examples over.

Track 140

Track 141

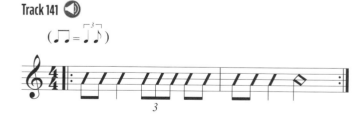

More Rhythms

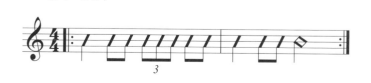

A/F#m from the 2nd to 12th Fret

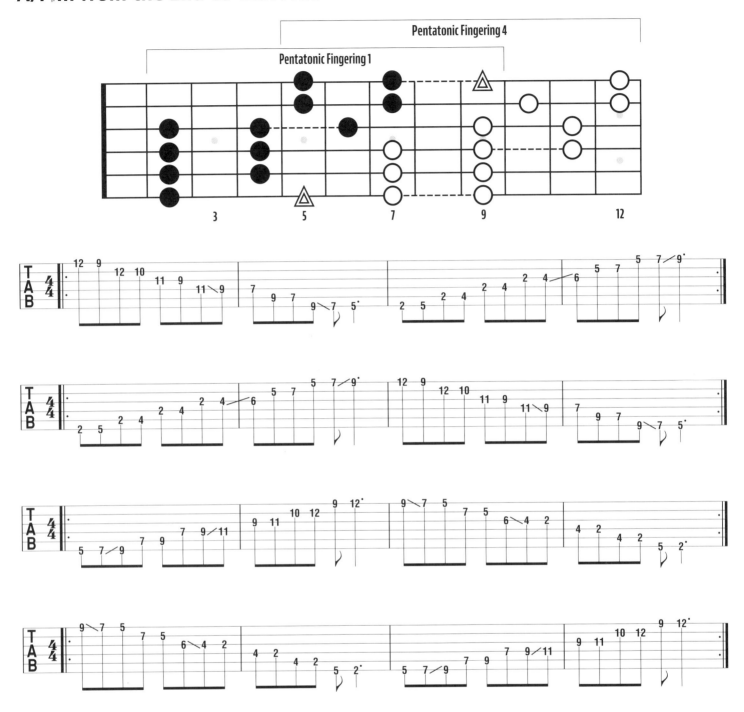

Use the audio player at **www.halleonard.com/mylibrary** and transpose any A, F# Minor, or G Blues Backing Track down a half step, then play the examples in that lower key.

Track 142

More Rhythms

Track 143

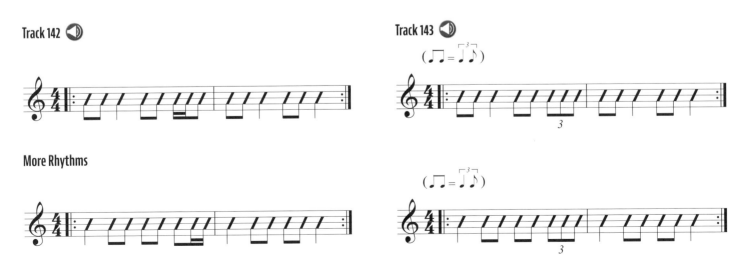

A/F#m from the 9th to 17th Fret

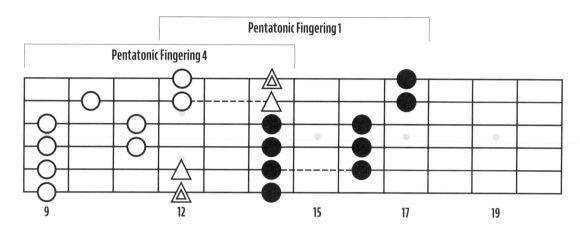

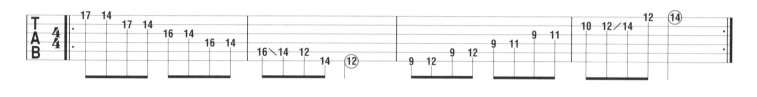

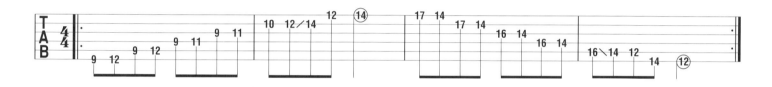

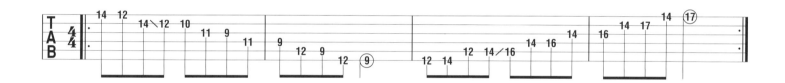

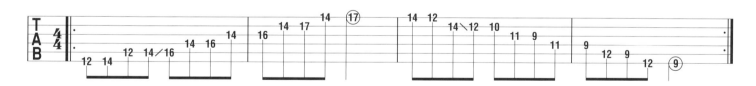

Use the audio player at **www.halleonard.com/mylibrary** and transpose any A, F# Minor, or G Blues Backing Track down a half step, then play the examples in that lower key.

Track 144

More Rhythms

Track 145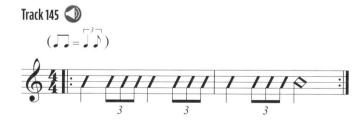

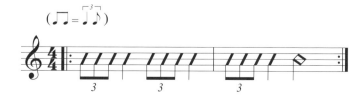

69

G/Em from Open Position to the 10th Fret

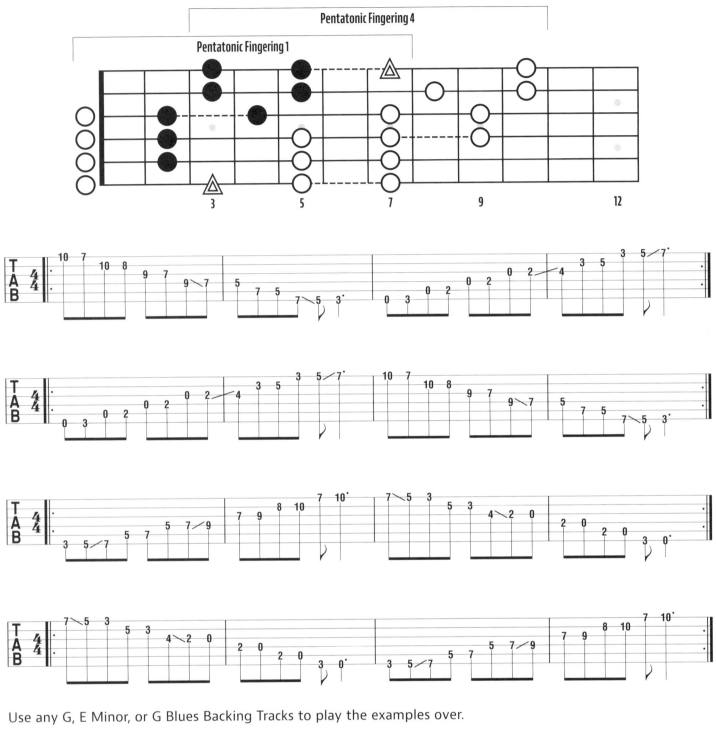

Use any G, E Minor, or G Blues Backing Tracks to play the examples over.

Track 146

Track 147

More Rhythms

G/Em from the 7th to 15th Fret

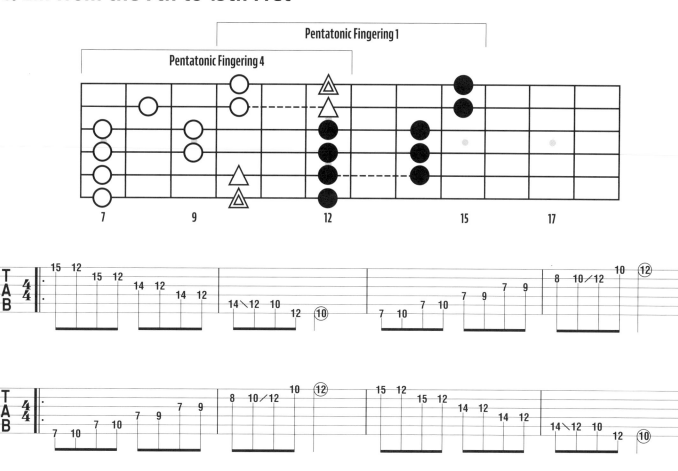

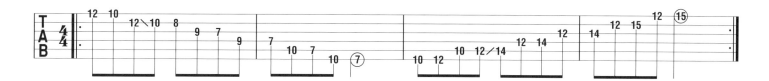

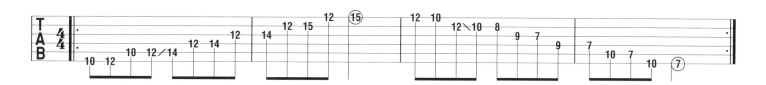

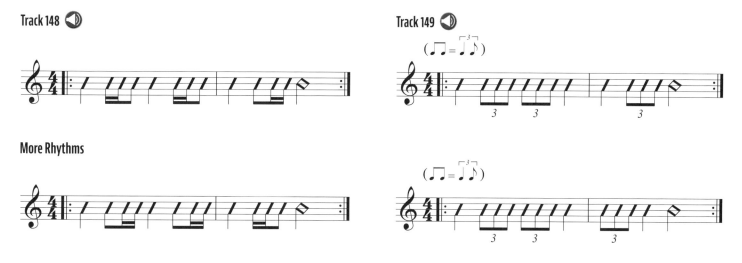

Use any G, E Minor, or G Blues Backing Tracks to play the examples over.

Track 148 🔊

Track 149 🔊

More Rhythms

G/Em from the 12th to 22nd Fret

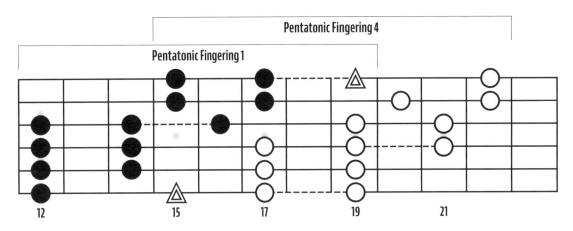

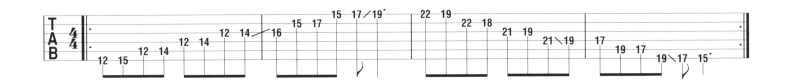

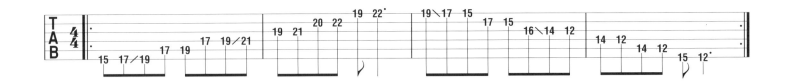

Use any G, E Minor, or G Blues Backing Tracks to play the examples over.

Track 150 🔊

More Rhythms

Track 151 🔊

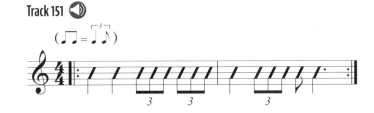

E/C♯m from the 4th to 12th Fret

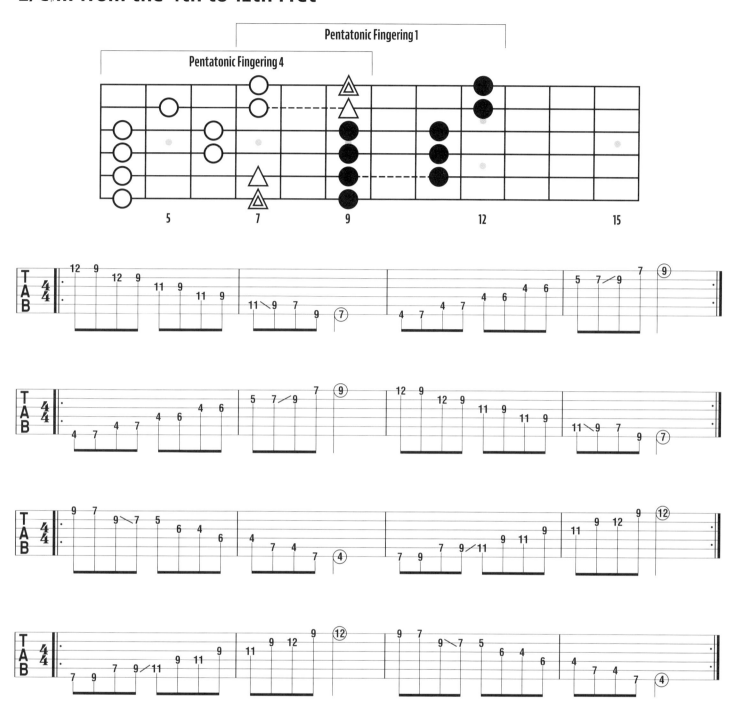

Use the audio player at **www.halleonard.com/mylibrary** and transpose any E, C♯ Minor, or D Blues Backing Track down a half step, then play the examples in that lower key.

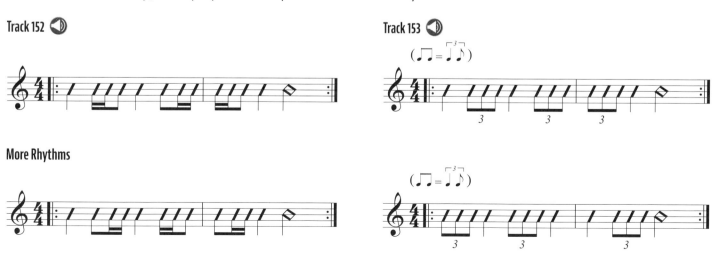

E/C♯m from the 9th to 19th Fret

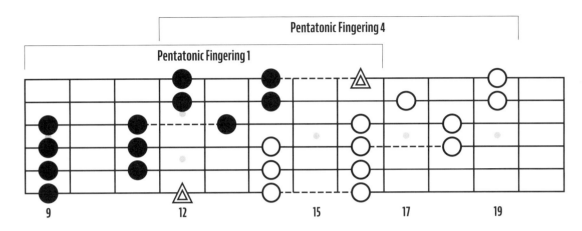

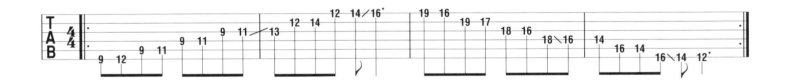

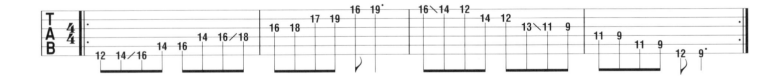

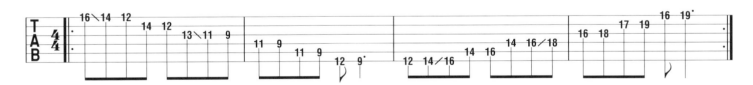

Use the audio player at **www.halleonard.com/mylibrary** and transpose any E, C♯ Minor, or D Blues Backing track down a half step, then play the examples in that lower key.

Track 154

More Rhythms

Track 155

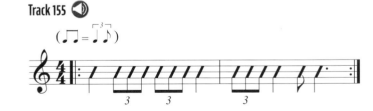

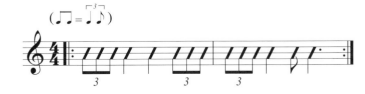

D/Bm from the 2nd to 10th Fret

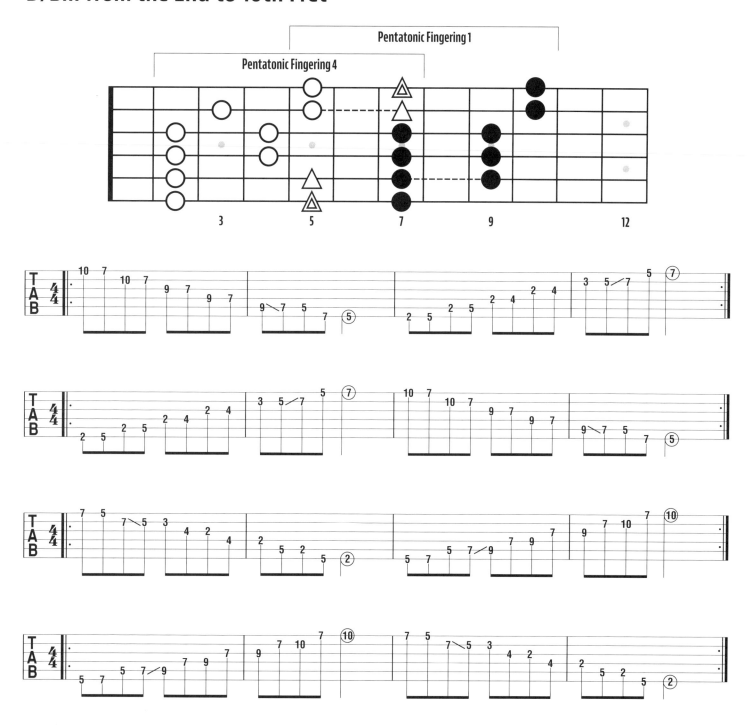

Use the audio player at **www.halleonard.com/mylibrary** and transpose any D, B Minor, or C Blues Backing track down a half step, then play the examples in that lower key.

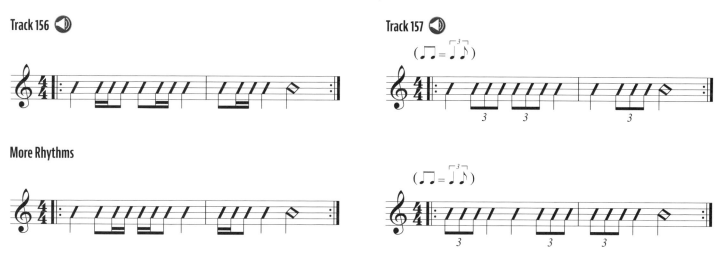

Track 156

Track 157

More Rhythms

D/Bm from the 7th to 17th Fret

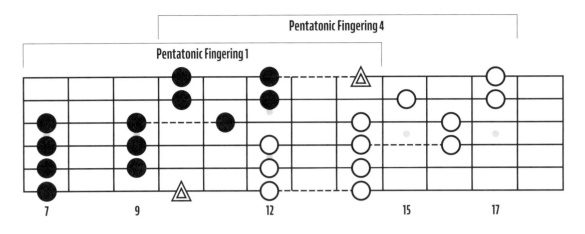

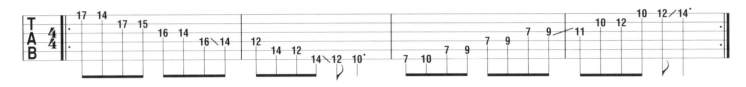

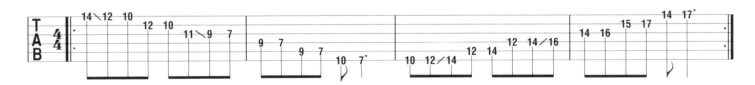

Use the audio player at **www.halleonard.com/mylibrary** and transpose any D, B Minor, or C Blues Backing track down a half step, then play the examples in that lower key.

Track 158 🔊

Track 159 🔊

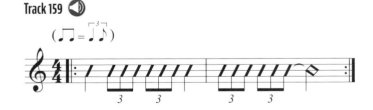

More Rhythms

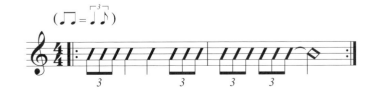

Chapter 6: Sixth-String-Root Major and Minor Scales with One-Position Fingerings

As you continue on your journey playing lead guitar, you will encounter situations where you'll want to expand the sound of the pentatonic scale and add new flavors. This can be accomplished by filling in the "flavor notes" around the pentatonic scale patterns you've already learned. There are three commonly used sounds we are going focus on: the major, natural minor, and Dorian scales. The term "one-position fingering" refers to the fact that your fretting hand will not shift at all while playing the scale. The root of the scale and its corresponding chord are located on string 6.

Let's start by examining what these scales have in common with the Pentatonic Fingering 1 you've already learned. As you try the examples below, observe where the pentatonic scale (the black dots) lies within the new fingerings. The white dots illuminate the new "flavor notes" we will work into our vocabulary.

Pentatonic Fingering 1

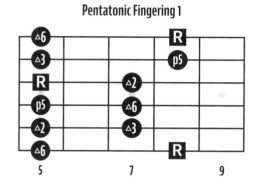

Major Scale

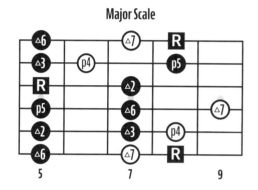

Standard Fingering

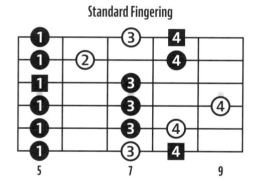

Alternate Fingering

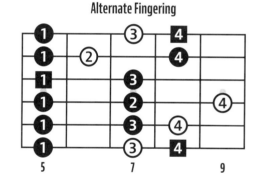

Play the following example to hear the major scale sound with its matching chord.

Track 160 🔊

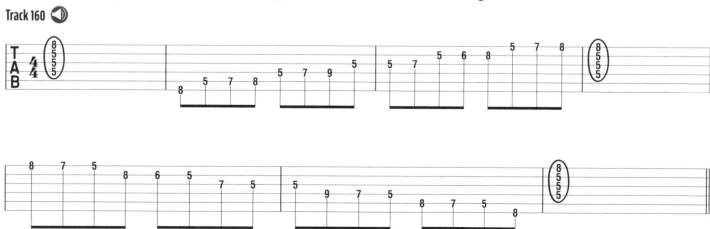

The Natural Minor Scale

The natural minor scale is created in the same way as the minor pentatonic scale: by taking the major scale and starting from its 6th step. Changing the starting note creates a new chord and sound from the exact same scale fingering. As you study and play the following fingerings, take notice of where the root notes have been relocated to and how the others relate to them.

Pentatonic Fingering 1

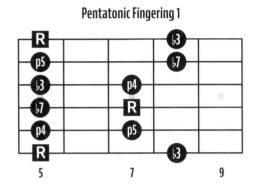

Natural Minor Scale

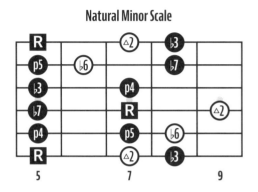

Standard Fingering

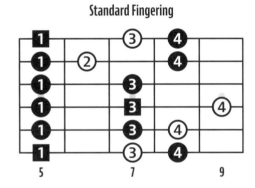

Alternate Fingering

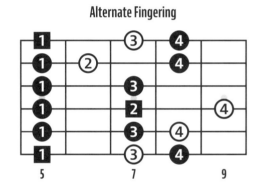

Play the following example to hear the natural minor scale sound with its matching chord.

Track 161

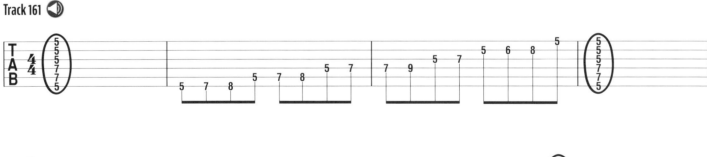

Descending Cells in the Key of C/Am

As we move forward, we will apply the same concept of moving our fingerings to different keys. Use the indicated fret number and corresponding audio track to transpose cells throughout the rest of the book.

First play the following phrases as written, then apply a rhythm from below or from the Appendix. Use the scale diagrams and corresponding audio track to change keys. Continue playing the rhythm and improvise your note choices using these backing tracks: C Major Backing Track 382 for Rhythm 1, C# Minor Backing Track 392 for Rhythm 2, D Major Backing Track 389 for Rhythm 3, and F# Minor Backing Track 394 for Rhythm 4.

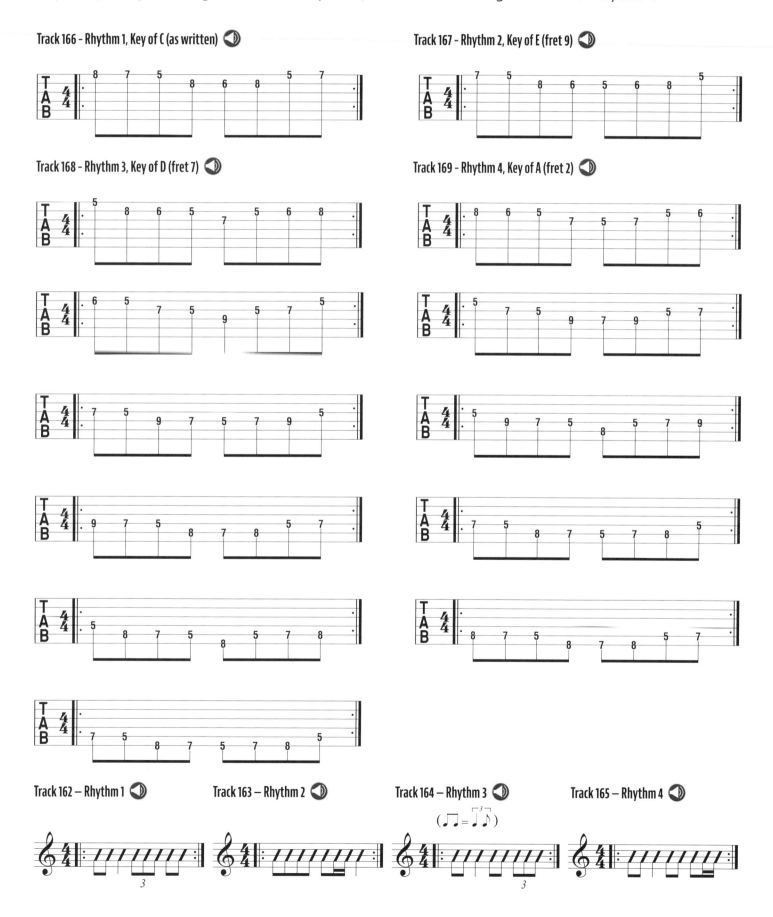

Track 166 - Rhythm 1, Key of C (as written)

Track 167 - Rhythm 2, Key of E (fret 9)

Track 168 - Rhythm 3, Key of D (fret 7)

Track 169 - Rhythm 4, Key of A (fret 2)

Track 162 – Rhythm 1

Track 163 – Rhythm 2

Track 164 – Rhythm 3

Track 165 – Rhythm 4

Ascending Cells in the Key of E/C♯m

Play the cell as written, then move it to the new key using the indicated fret number as your guide. Apply a rhythm from below or from the Appendix. Use the scale diagrams and corresponding audio track to change keys. Continue playing the rhythm and improvise your note choices using these backing tracks: C Major Backing Track 382 for Rhythm 1, C♯ Minor Backing Track 392 for Rhythm 2, D Major Backing Track 389 for Rhythm 3, and F♯ Minor Backing Track 394 for Rhythm 4.

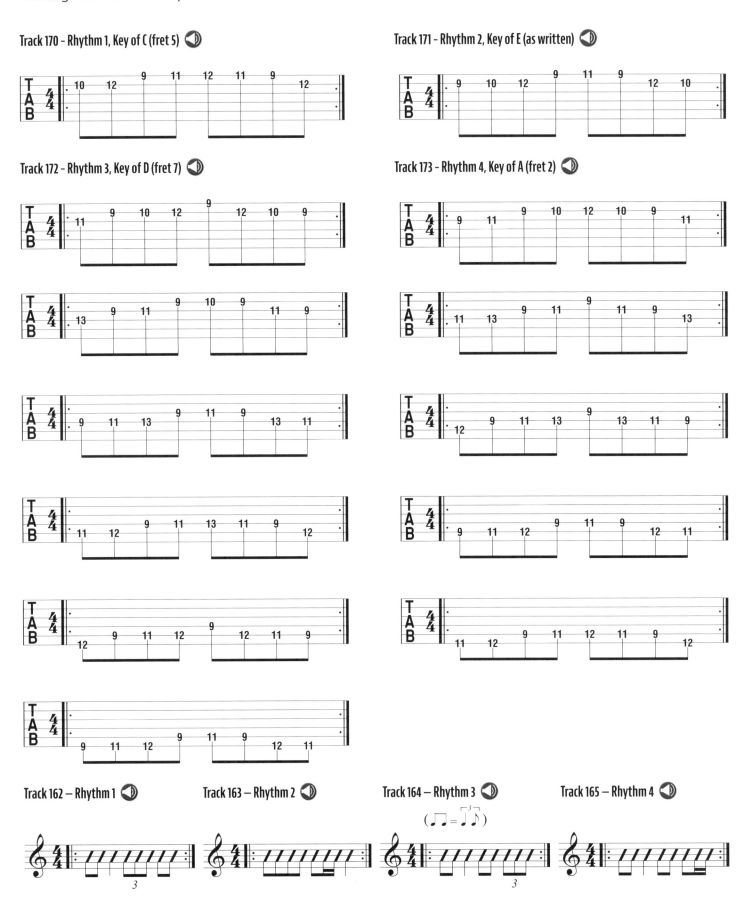

Descending Cells Connected in the Key of D/Bm

Track 174 - Rhythm 3

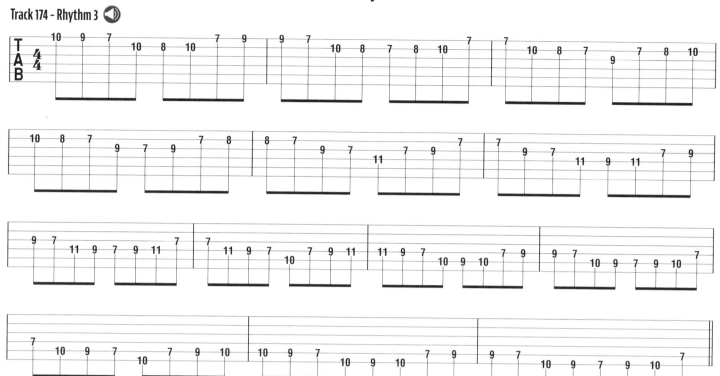

Ascending Cells Connected in the Key of A/F#m

Track 175 - Rhythm 4

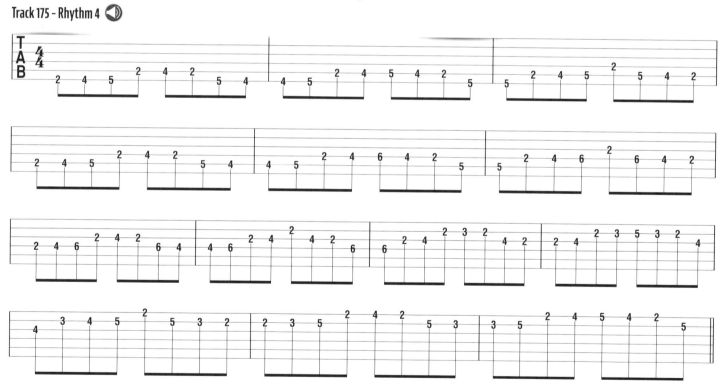

When you can play these easily, take the guide away and use: C Major Backing Track 382 for Rhythm 1, C# Minor Backing Track 392 for Rhythm 2, D Major Backing Track 389 for Rhythm 3, and F# Minor Backing Track 394 for Rhythm 4. More rhythms can be found in the Appendix.

Track 162 – Rhythm 1   Track 163 – Rhythm 2   Track 164 – Rhythm 3   Track 165 – Rhythm 4

Solo 17: C/Am

Track 176 🔊   Backing Track 382 🔊

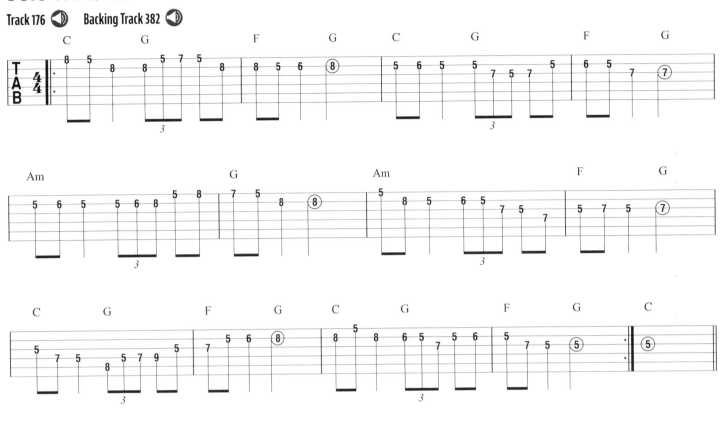

Solo 18: E/C#m

Track 177 🔊   Backing Track 392 🔊

Solo 19: D/Bm

Track 178 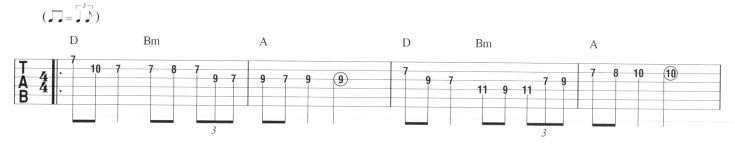 Backing Track 389

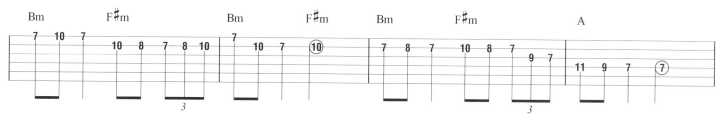

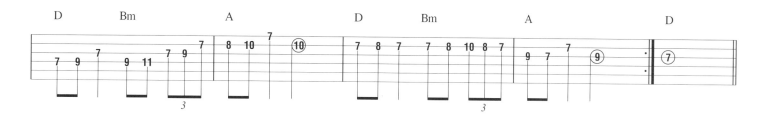

Solo 20: A/F#m

Track 179 Backing Track 394

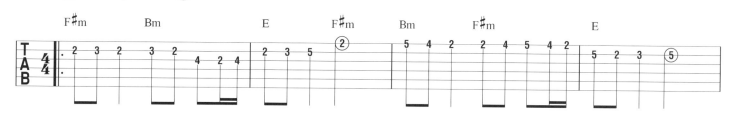

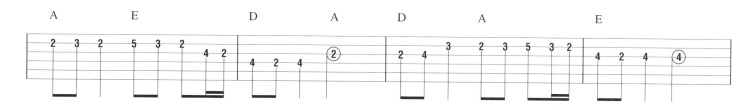

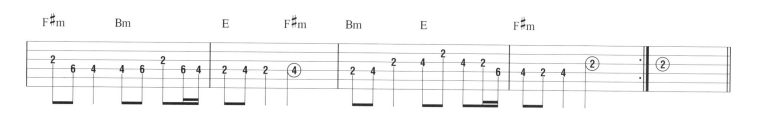

Chapter 7: Sixth-String-Root Dorian Scales with One-Position Fingerings

The Dorian scale (or mode) is very similar to the natural minor scale, but changes the 6th degree of the scale from a minor to major interval. The result is a brighter-sounding minor scale that can be used in blues and other compatible chord progressions. In the same way as before, we will add the white dots to our existing Pentatonic Fingering 1 to highlight the new flavors in our vocabulary.

Pentatonic Fingering 1

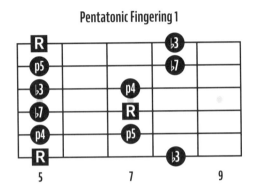

Dorian Scale

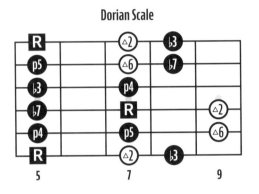

Standard Fingering

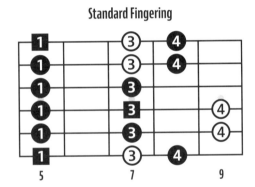

Alternate Fingering

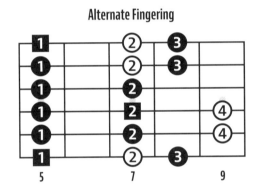

Play the following exercise to hear the Dorian scale with its matching chord, and pay extra attention to the sound of the major 6th.

Track 180 🔊

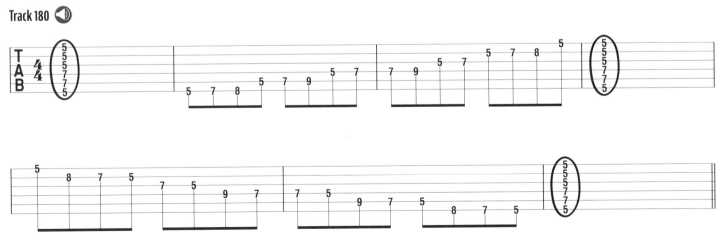

Descending Cells in A Dorian

Play the cell as written, then move it to the new tonal center using the indicated fret number as your guide. Apply a rhythm from below or from the Appendix. Use the scale diagrams and corresponding audio track to change keys. Continue playing the rhythm and improvise your note choices using these backing tracks: A Blues Backing Track 403 for Rhythm 1, C Dorian Backing Track 404 for Rhythm 2, G Blues Backing Track 400 for Rhythm 3, and D Dorian Backing Track 405 for Rhythm 4.

Track 185 - Rhythm 1, Key of Am (as written)

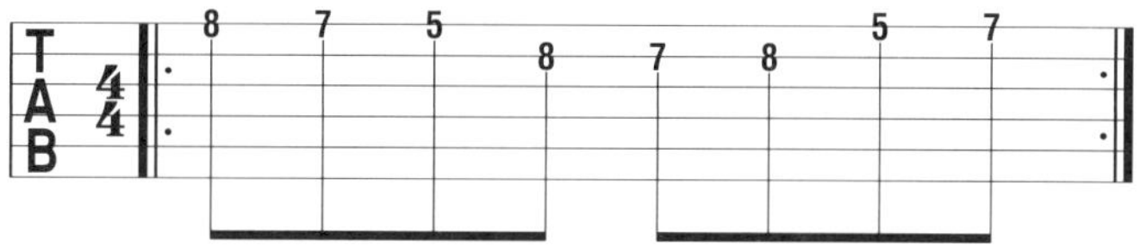

Track 186 - Rhythm 2, Key of Cm (fret 8)

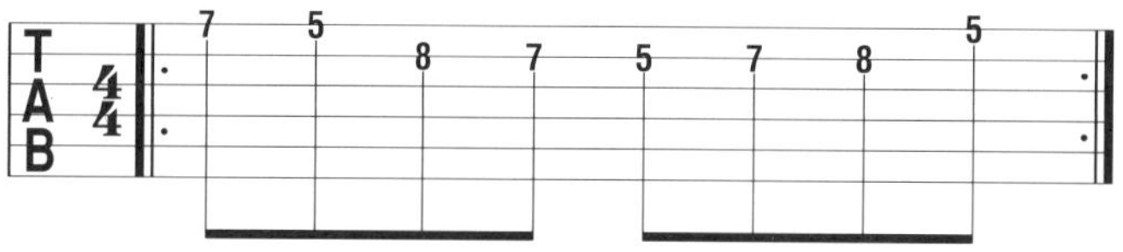

Track 187 - Rhythm 3, Key of Gm (fret 3)

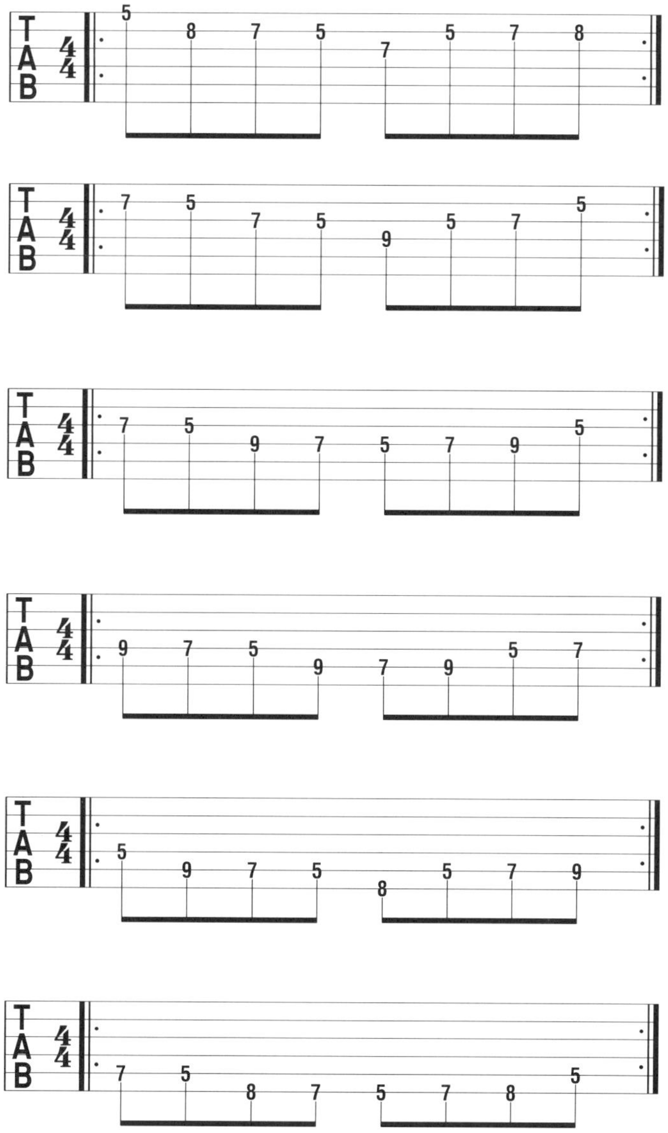

Track 188 - Rhythm 4, Key of Dm (fret 10)

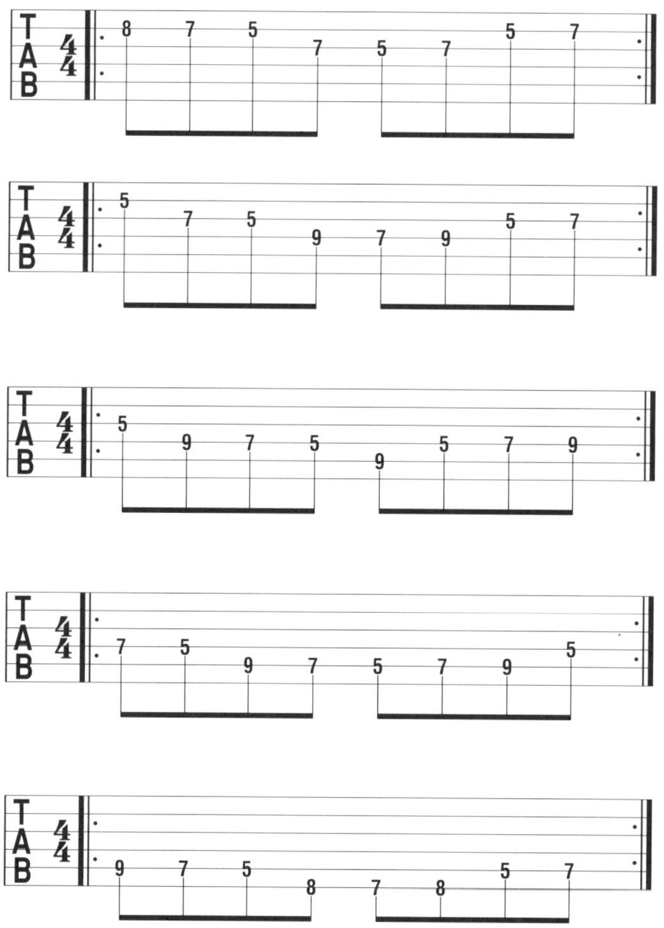

Track 181 – Rhythm 1

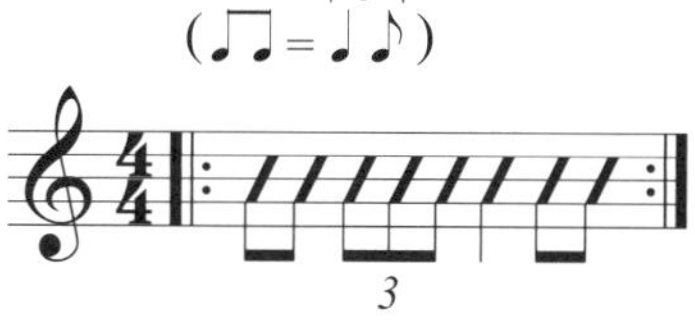

Track 182 – Rhythm 2

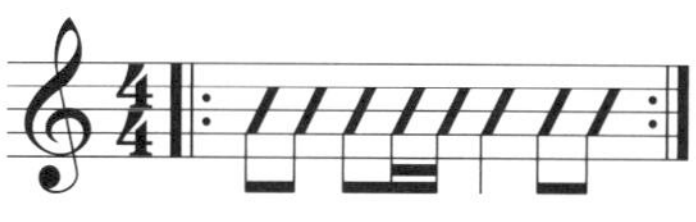

Track 183 – Rhythm 3

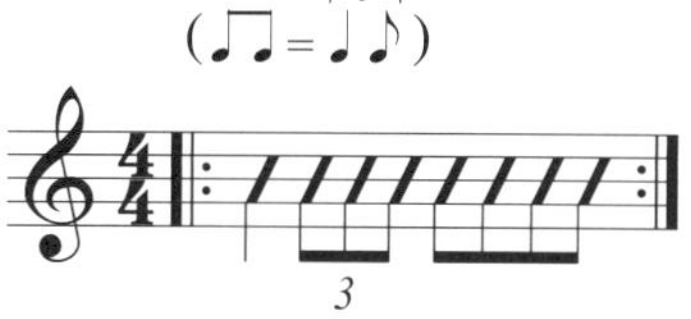

Track 184 – Rhythm 4

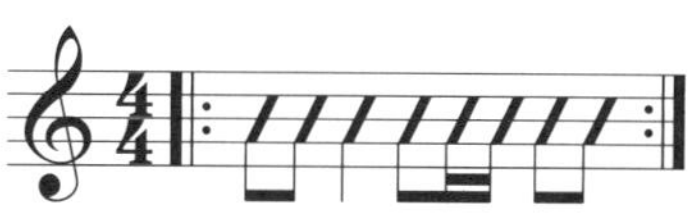

Ascending Cells in C Dorian

Play the cell as written, then move it to the new tonal center using the indicated fret number as your guide. Apply a rhythm from below or from the Appendix. Use the scale diagrams and corresponding audio track to change keys. Continue playing the rhythm and improvise your note choices using these backing tracks: A Blues Backing Track 403 for Rhythm 1, C Dorian Backing Track 404 for Rhythm 2, G Blues Backing Track 400 for Rhythm 3, and D Dorian Backing Track 405 for Rhythm 4.

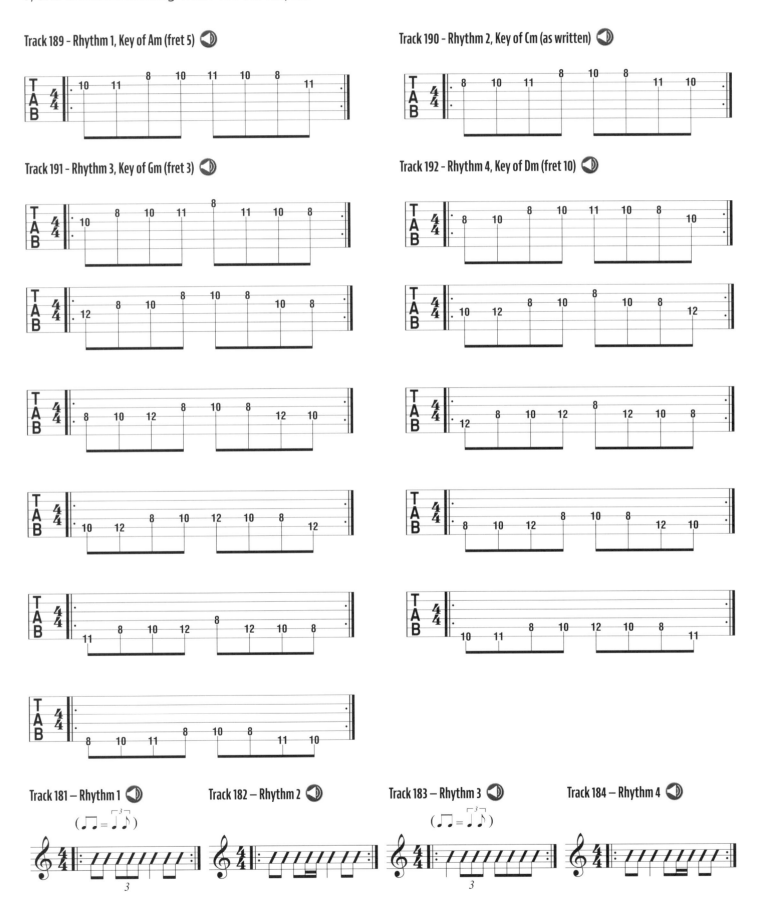

Descending Cells Connected in G Dorian

Track 193 – Rhythm 3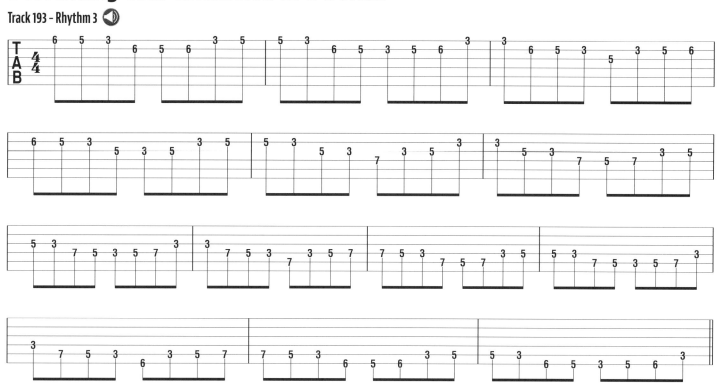

Ascending Cells Connected in D Dorian

Track 194 – Rhythm 4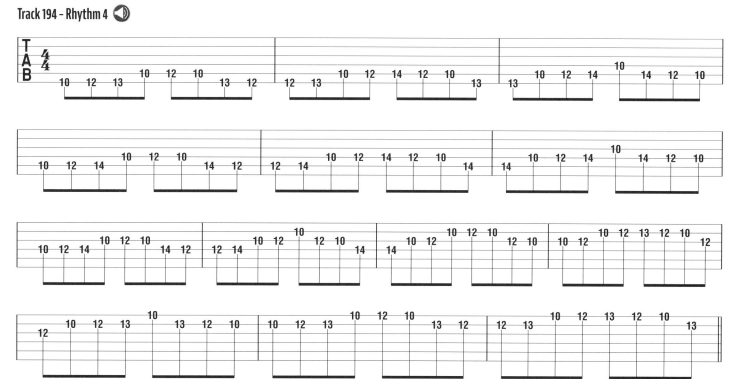

When you can play these easily, take the guide away and use: A Blues Backing Track 403 for Rhythm 1, C Dorian Backing Track 404 for Rhythm 2, G Blues Backing Track 400 for Rhythm 3, and D Dorian Backing Track 405 for Rhythm 4. More rhythms can be found in the Appendix.

Track 181 – Rhythm 1   Track 182 – Rhythm 2   Track 183 – Rhythm 3   Track 184 – Rhythm 4

Solo 21: A Dorian

Track 195 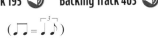 Backing Track 403

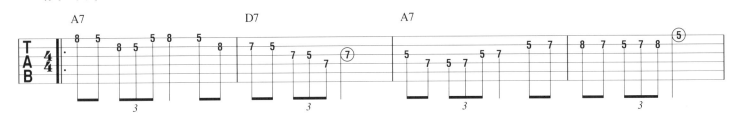

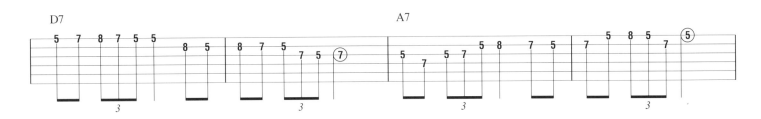

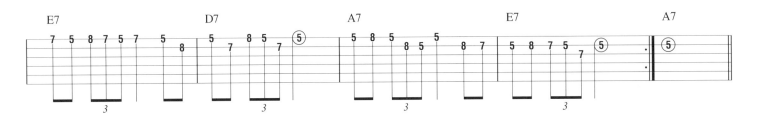

Solo 22: C Dorian

Track 196 Backing Track 404

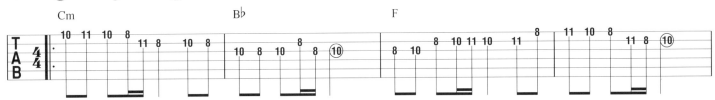

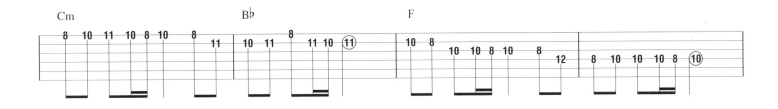

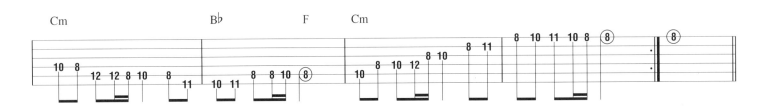

Solo 23: G Dorian

Track 197 Backing Track 400

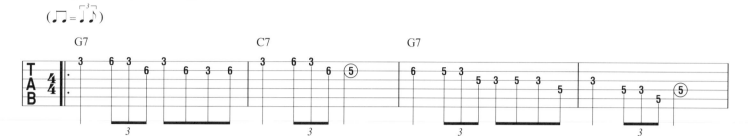

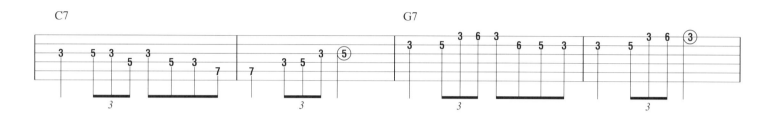

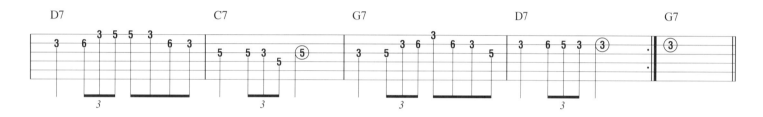

Solo 24: D Dorian

Track 198 Backing Track 405

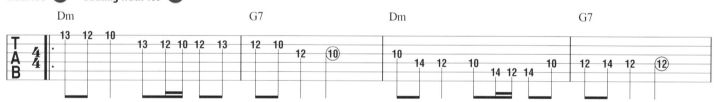

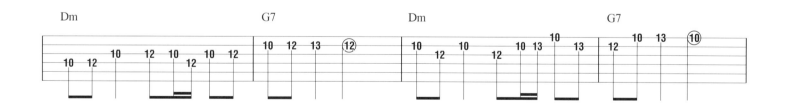

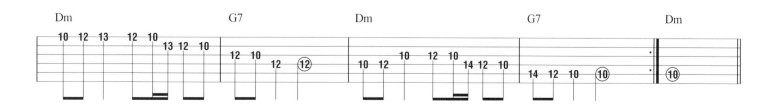

Chapter 8: Sixth-String-Root Lower-Diagonal Major and Minor Scales with Three-Notes-Per-String Fingerings

In practicing the previous chapters, you may have noticed that all the one-position fingerings have something in common. Each fingering contains one string that has two notes on it while the others have three. It is very common that guitarists use a position shift to keep three notes on each string. Doing so offers some useful advantages when playing patterns that move across strings. One is that you can keep a pattern going without having to alter it when you encounter a string with two notes on it. Another is that it enables you to easily shift between the diagonal pentatonic fingering and the full major or minor scale.

The term "lower" is used to describe the direction that we are shifting positions. The six highest notes of the scale pattern are the same, and our new fingering moves diagonally down the neck in relation to the one-position fingering. While examining the black dots, observe how they cover the "lower" portion of the diagonal pentatonic scale and make it a great place to switch between the sounds of each scale.

One-Position Fingering   Lower-Diagonal Fingering

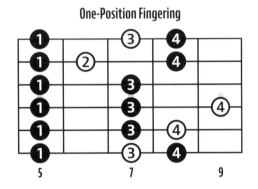

Lower-Diagonal Major Intervals   Lower-Diagonal Minor Intervals

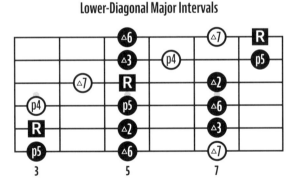
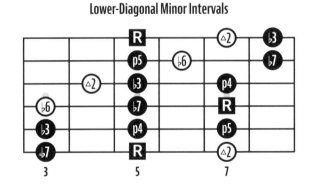

Play the following exercises below while paying attention to the fingerings to help get used to shifting positions.

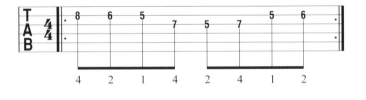
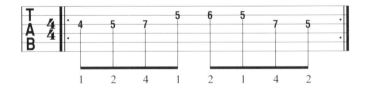

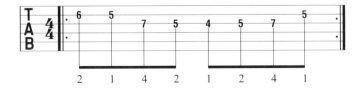
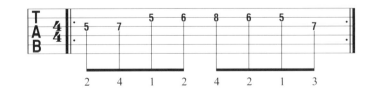

Descending Cells in the Key of E/C#m

Play the cell as written, then move it to the new key using the indicated fret number as your guide. Apply a rhythm from below or from the Appendix. Use the scale diagrams and corresponding audio track to change keys. Continue playing the rhythm and improvise your note choices using these backing tracks: E Backing Track 385 for Rhythm 1, C Backing Track 390 for Rhythm 2, E Minor Backing Track 396 for Rhythm 3, and B Minor Backing Track 397 for Rhythm 4.

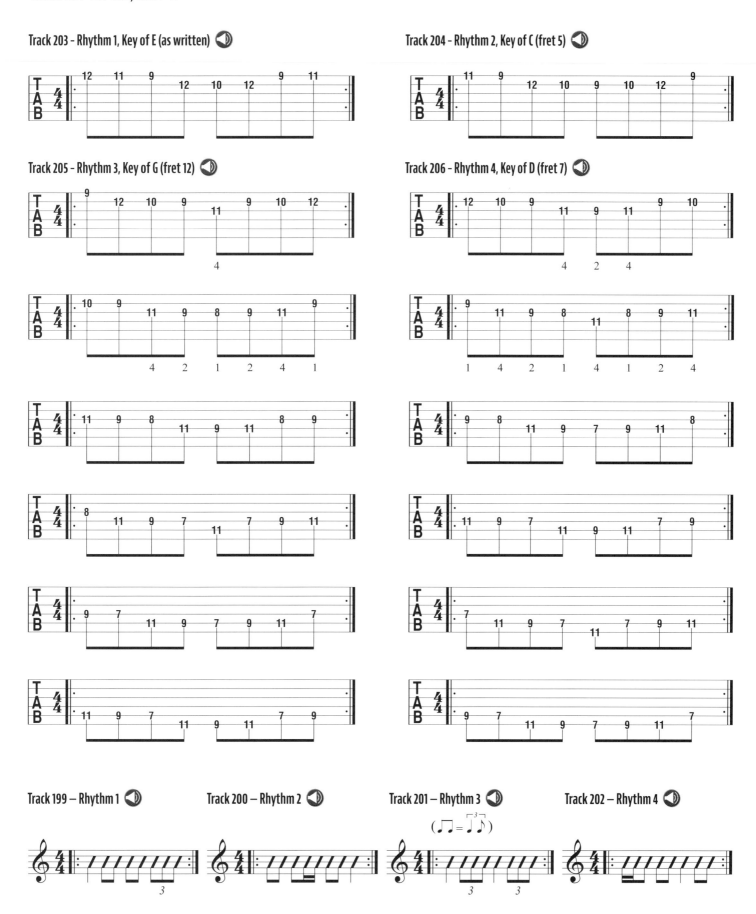

Ascending Cells in the Key of C/Am

Play the cell as written, then move it to the new key using the indicated fret number as your guide. Apply a rhythm from below or from the Appendix. Use the scale diagrams and corresponding audio track to change keys. Continue playing the rhythm and improvise your note choices using these backing tracks: E Backing Track 385 for Rhythm 1, C Backing Track 390 for Rhythm 2, E Minor Backing Track 396 for Rhythm 3, and B Minor Backing Track 397 for Rhythm 4.

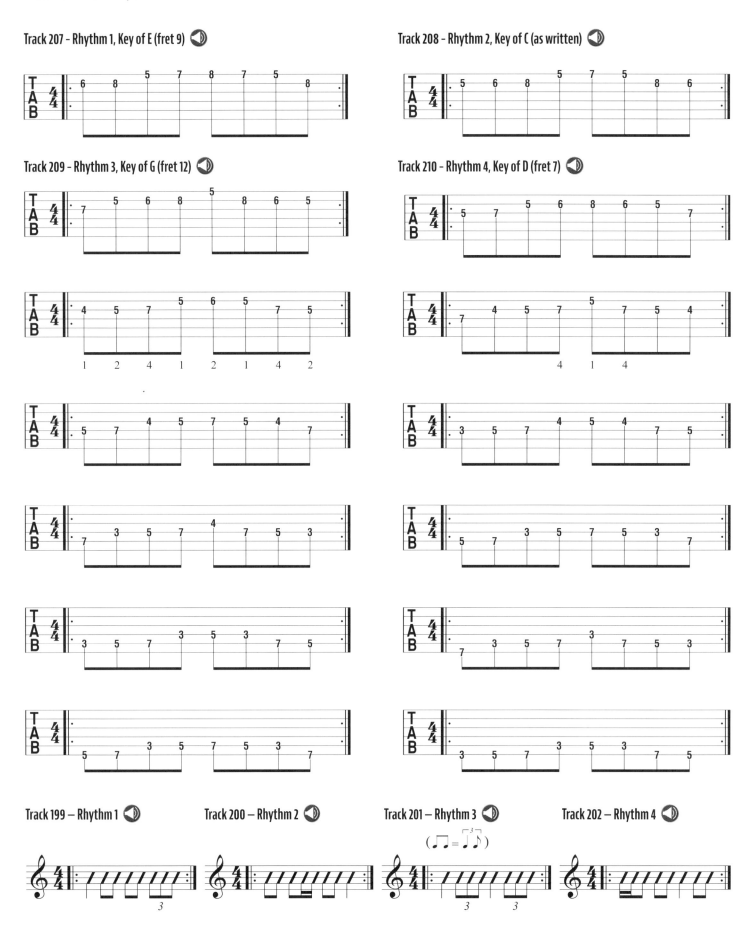

Descending Cells Connected in the Key of G/Em

Track 211 - Rhythm 3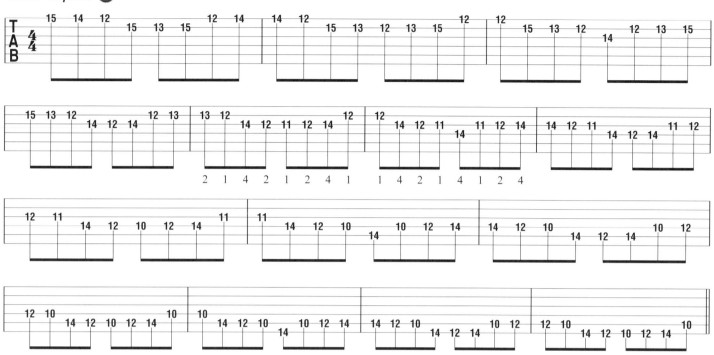

Ascending Cells Connected in the Key of D/Bm

Track 212 - Rhythm 4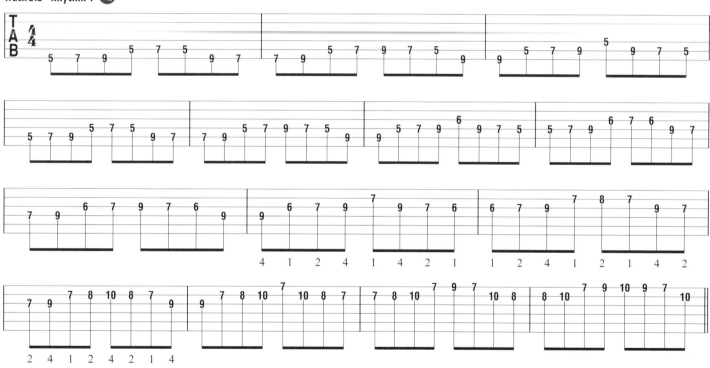

When you can play these easily, take the guide away and use: E Backing Track 385 for Rhythm 1, C Backing Track 390 for Rhythm 2, E Minor Backing Track 396 for Rhythm 3, and B Minor Backing Track 397 for Rhythm 4. More rhythms can be found in the Appendix.

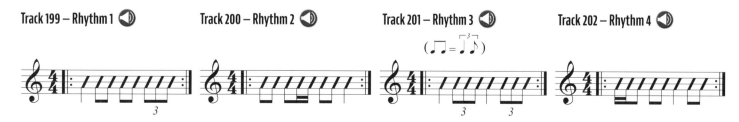

Track 199 – Rhythm 1   Track 200 – Rhythm 2   Track 201 – Rhythm 3   Track 202 – Rhythm 4

Solo 25: E/C#m

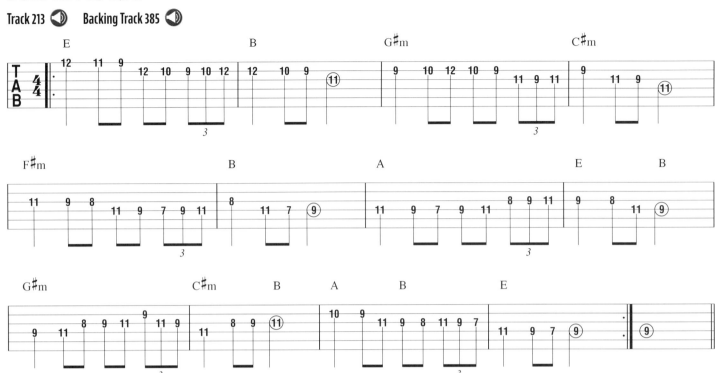

Track 213   Backing Track 385

Solo 26: C/Am

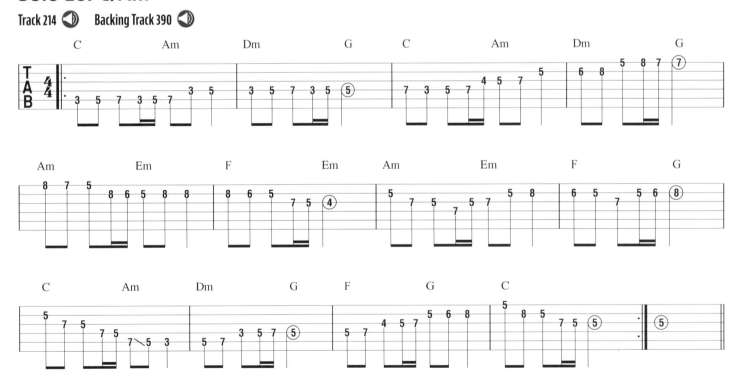

Track 214   Backing Track 390

94

Solo 27: G/Em

Track 215 🔊   Backing Track 396 🔊

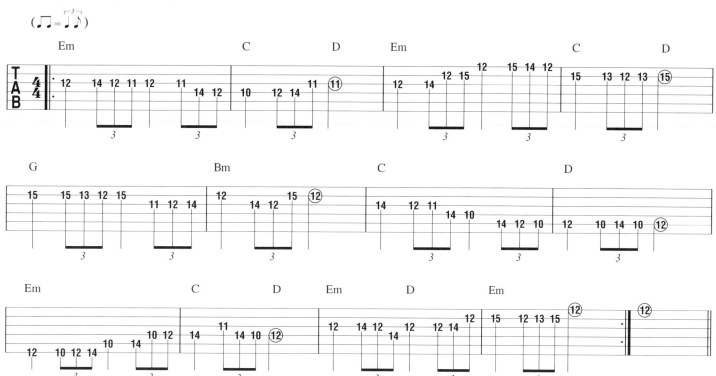

Solo 28: D/Bm

Track 216 🔊   Backing Track 397 🔊

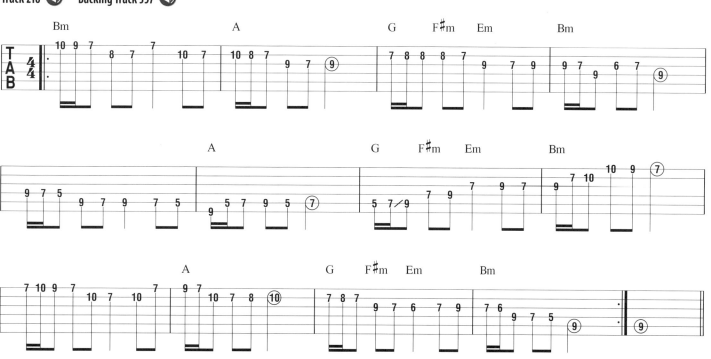

Chapter 9: Sixth-String-Root Lower-Diagonal Dorian Scales with Three-Notes-Per-String Fingerings

The concept of using a position shift to keep the three-notes-per-string fingering can be applied to many scales, including Dorian. Remember to visualize the "lower" portion of Diagonal Pentatonic Fingering 1 using the black dots, and to think of the white dots as added color notes to spice up your lead playing.

One-Position Fingering

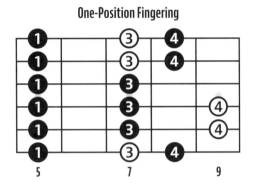

Lower-Diagonal Fingering

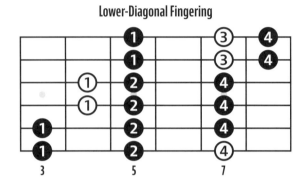

One-Position Intervals

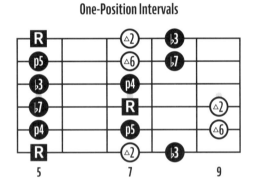

Lower-Diagonal Intervals

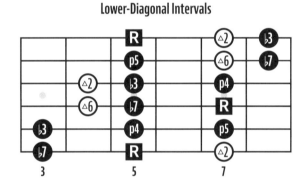

Play the following exercises while paying attention to the fingerings to help get used to shifting positions. Try applying rhythms to them as well. It is always a great benefit.

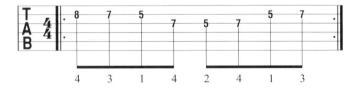

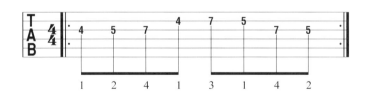

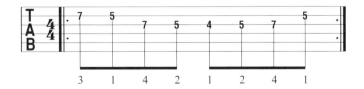

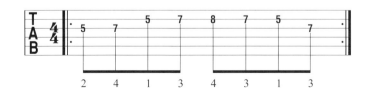

Descending Cells in A Dorian

Play the cell as written, then move it to the new tonal center using the indicated fret number as your guide. Apply a rhythm from below or from the Appendix. Use the scale diagrams and corresponding audio track to change keys. Continue playing the rhythm and improvise your note choices using these backing tracks: A Blues Backing Track 403 for Rhythm 1, C Dorian Backing Track 406 for Rhythm 2, G Blues Backing Track 400 for Rhythm 3, and D Dorian Backing Track 407 for Rhythm 4.

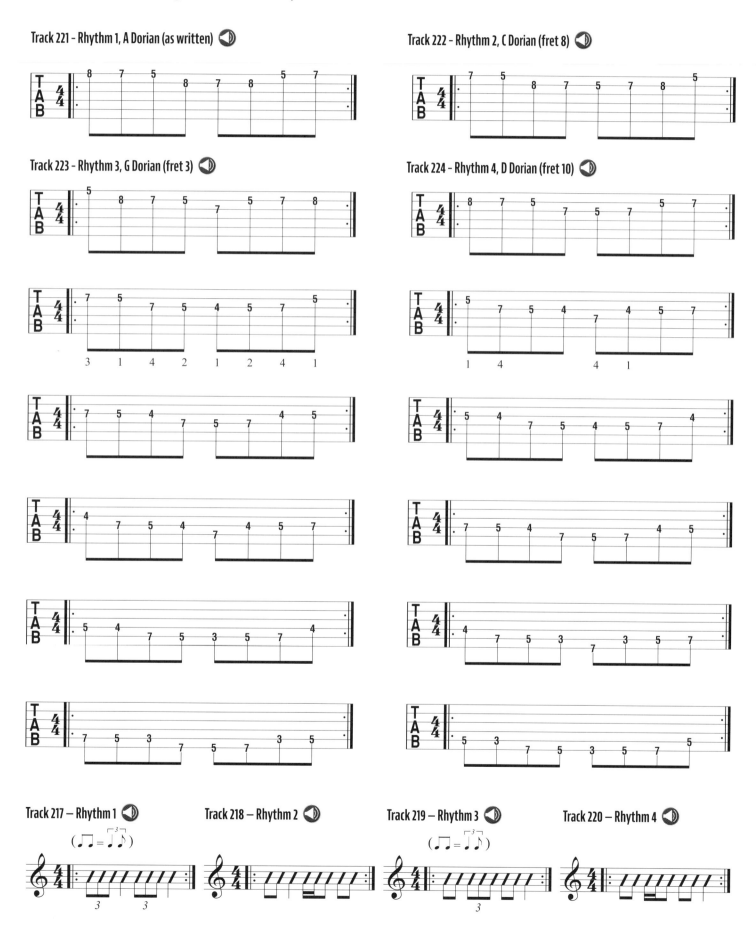

Track 221 – Rhythm 1, A Dorian (as written)

Track 222 – Rhythm 2, C Dorian (fret 8)

Track 223 – Rhythm 3, G Dorian (fret 3)

Track 224 – Rhythm 4, D Dorian (fret 10)

Track 217 – Rhythm 1

Track 218 – Rhythm 2

Track 219 – Rhythm 3

Track 220 – Rhythm 4

Ascending Cells in C Dorian

Play the cell as written, then move it to the new tonal center using the indicated fret number as your guide. Apply a rhythm from below or from the Appendix. Use the scale diagrams and corresponding audio track to change keys. Continue playing the rhythm and improvise your note choices using these backing tracks: A Blues Backing Track 403 for Rhythm 1, C Dorian Backing Track 406 for Rhythm 2, G Blues Backing Track 400 for Rhythm 3, and D Dorian Backing Track 407 for Rhythm 4.

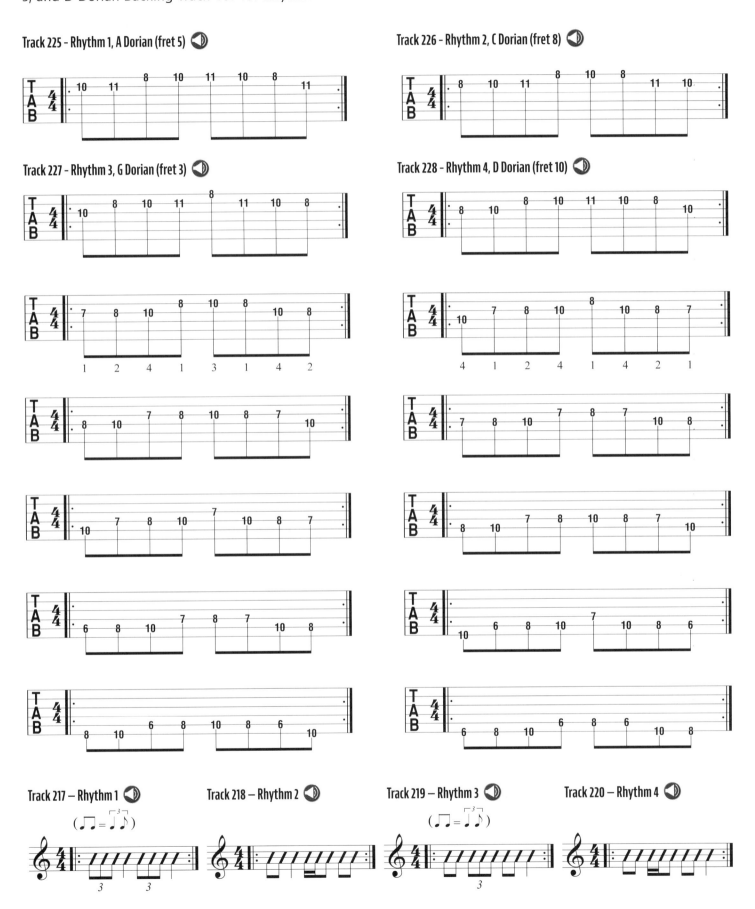

Descending Cells Connected in G Dorian

Track 229 - Rhythm 3

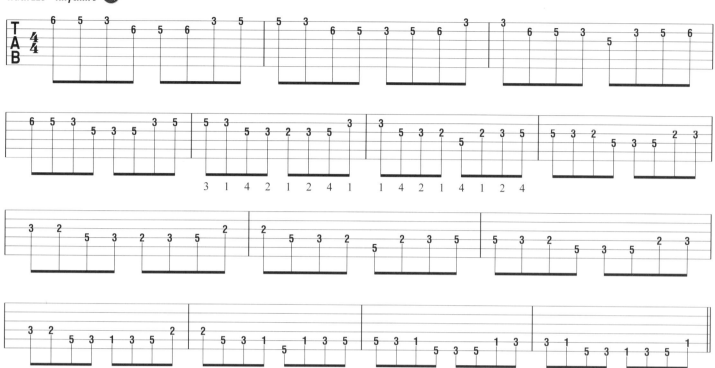

Ascending Cells Connected in D Dorian

Track 230 - Rhythm 4

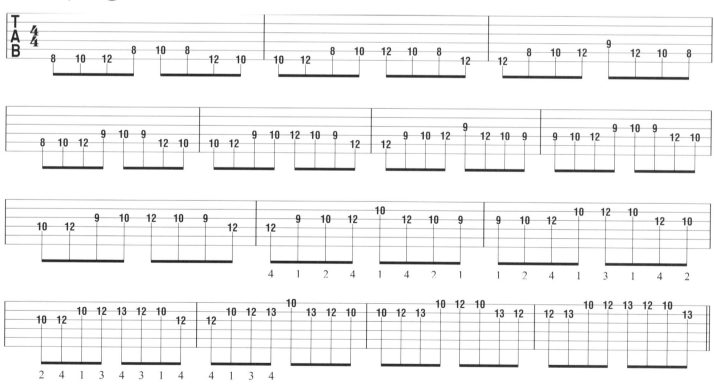

When you can play these easily, take the guide away and use: A Blues Backing Track 403 for Rhythm 1, C Dorian Backing Track 406 for Rhythm 2, G Blues Backing Track 400 for Rhythm 3, and D Dorian Backing Track 407 for Rhythm 4. More rhythms can be found in the Appendix.

Track 217 – Rhythm 1   Track 218 – Rhythm 2   Track 219 – Rhythm 3   Track 220 – Rhythm 4

Solo 29: A Dorian

Track 231   Backing Track 403

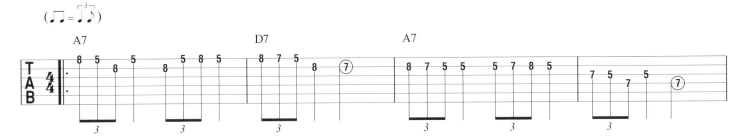

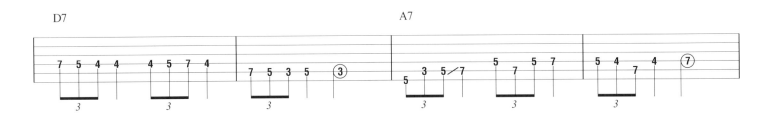

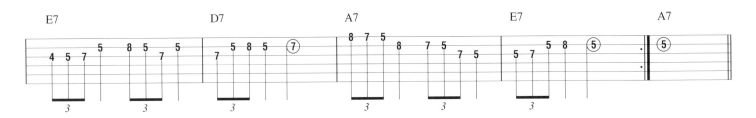

Solo 30: C Dorian

Track 232   Backing Track 406

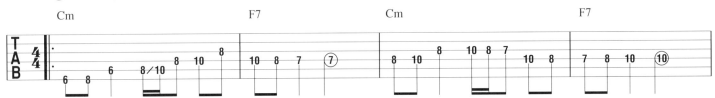

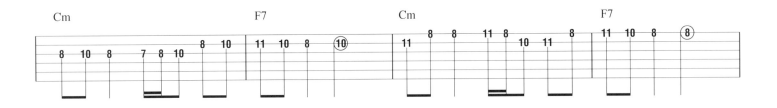

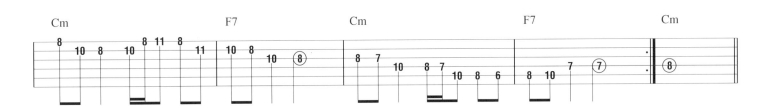

Solo 31: G Dorian

Track 233   Backing Track 400

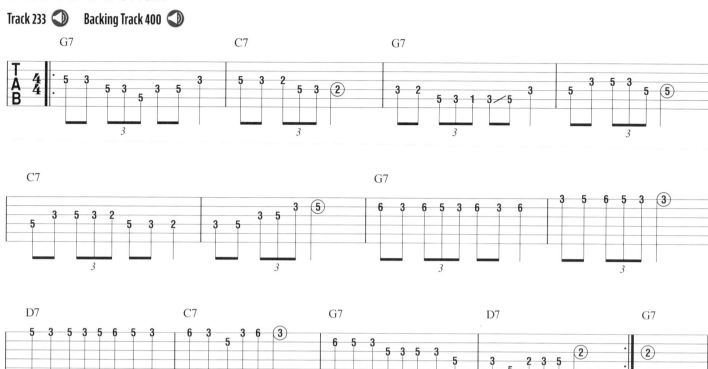

Solo 32: D Dorian

Track 234   Backing Track 407

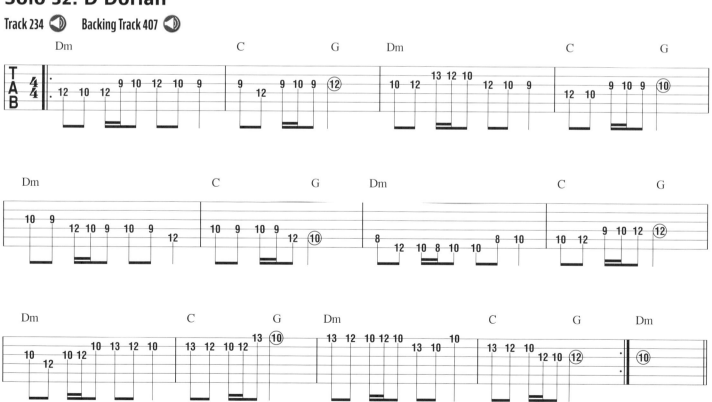

Chapter 10: Sixth-String-Root Upper-Diagonal Major and Minor Scales with Three-Notes-Per-String Fingerings

Now that we have introduced the idea of shifting positions to keep the three-notes-per-string fingering, let's expand our one-position major and minor fingering to cover the upper portion of Diagonal Pentatonic Fingering 1. Visualize the upper portion of the pentatonic with the black dots and the full-scale color notes that are nearby with the white dots.

One-Position Fingering

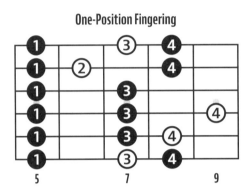

Upper-Diagonal Fingering

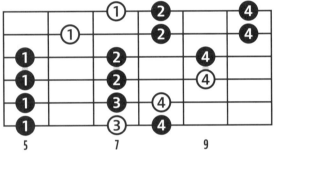

Upper-Diagonal Alternate Fingering

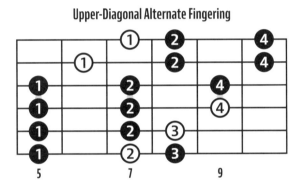

Upper-Diagonal Major Intervals

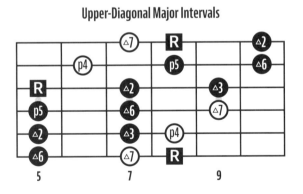

Upper-Diagonal Minor Intervals

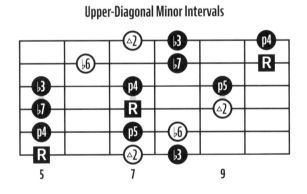

Try applying rhythms to the exercises below as you get used to the position shifts.

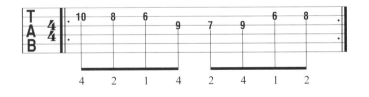

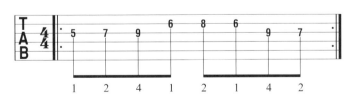

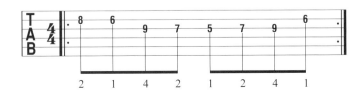

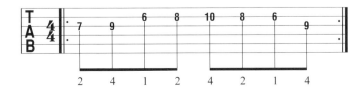

Descending Cells in the Key of C/Am

Play the cell as written, then move it to the new key using the indicated fret number as your guide. Apply a rhythm from below or from the Appendix. Use the scale diagrams and corresponding audio track to change keys. Continue playing the rhythm and improvise your note choices using these backing tracks: C Backing Track 390 for Rhythm 1, A Backing Track 387 for Rhythm 2, C♯ Minor Backing Track 393 for Rhythm 3, and D Backing Track 388 for Rhythm 4.

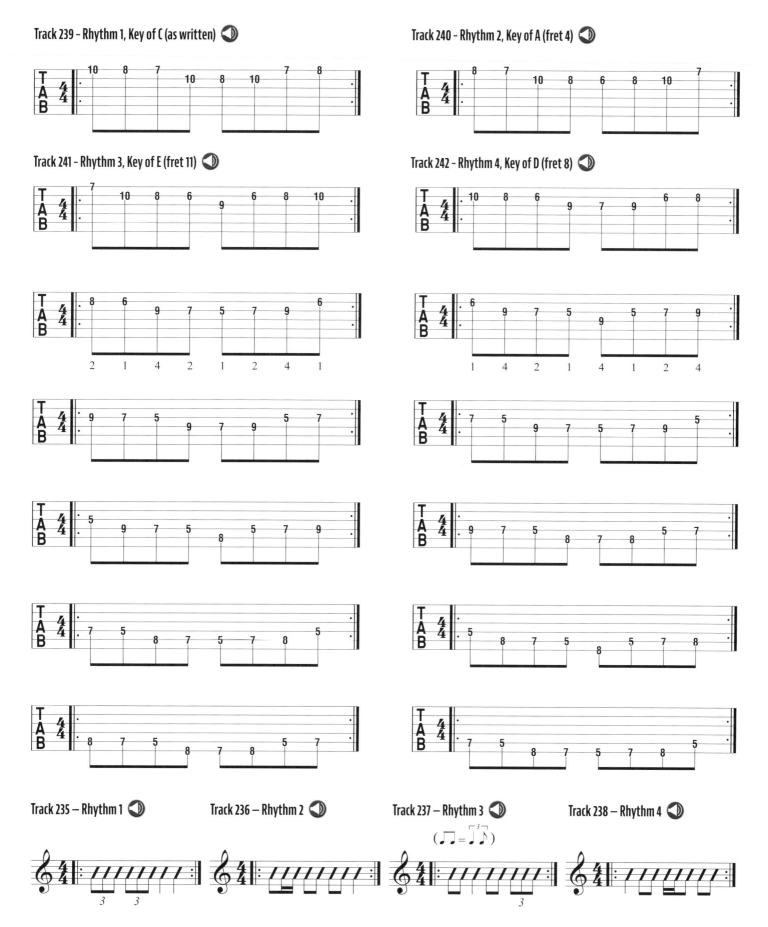

Ascending Cells in the Key of A/F♯m

Play the cell as written, then move it to the new key using the indicated fret number as your guide. Apply a rhythm from below or from the Appendix. Use the scale diagrams and corresponding audio track to change keys. Continue playing the rhythm and improvise your note choices using these backing tracks: C Backing Track 390 for Rhythm 1, A Backing Track 387 for Rhythm 2, C♯ Minor Backing Track 393 for Rhythm 3, and D Backing Track 388 for Rhythm 4.

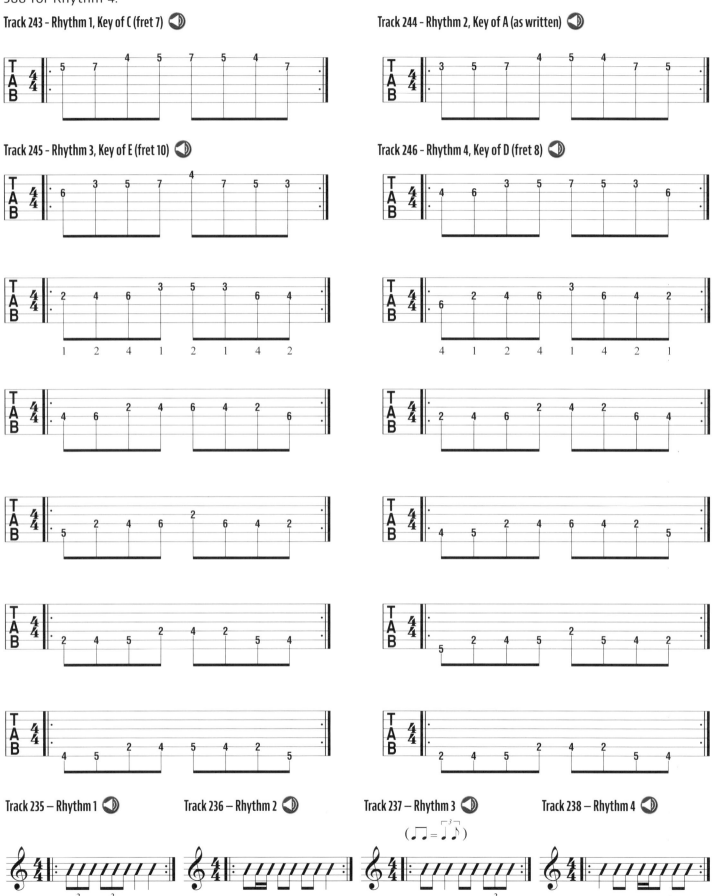

Track 243 - Rhythm 1, Key of C (fret 7)

Track 244 - Rhythm 2, Key of A (as written)

Track 245 - Rhythm 3, Key of E (fret 10)

Track 246 - Rhythm 4, Key of D (fret 8)

Track 235 – Rhythm 1   **Track 236 – Rhythm 2**   **Track 237 – Rhythm 3**   **Track 238 – Rhythm 4**

Descending Cells Connected in the Key of E/C♯m

Track 247 – Rhythm 3

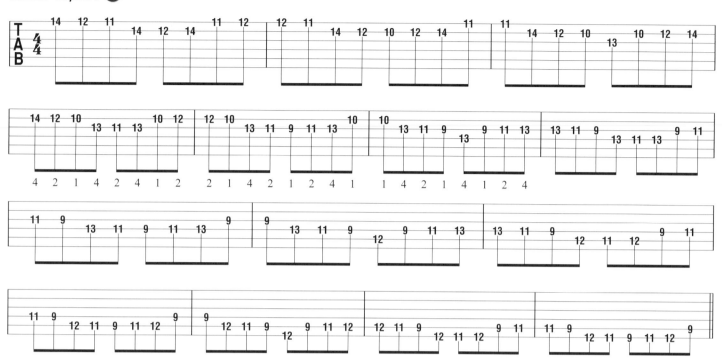

Ascending Cells Connected in the Key of D/Bm

Track 248 – Rhythm 4

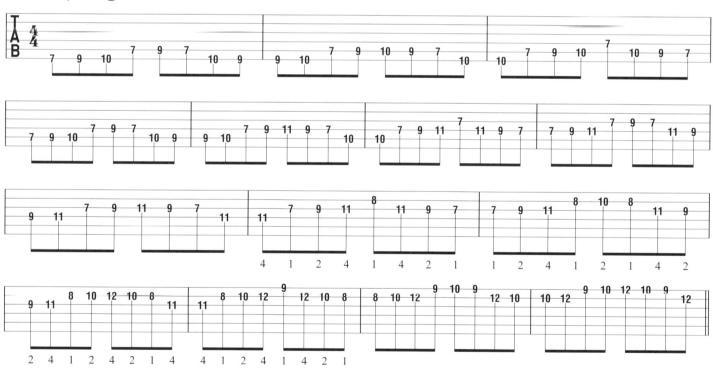

When you can play these easily, take the guide away and use: C Backing Track 390 for Rhythm 1, A Backing Track 387 for Rhythm 2, C♯ Minor Backing Track 393 for Rhythm 3, and D Backing Track 388 for Rhythm 4. More rhythms can be found in the Appendix.

Track 235 – Rhythm 1   Track 236 – Rhythm 2   Track 237 – Rhythm 3   Track 238 – Rhythm 4

Solo 33: C/Am

Track 249  Backing Track 390

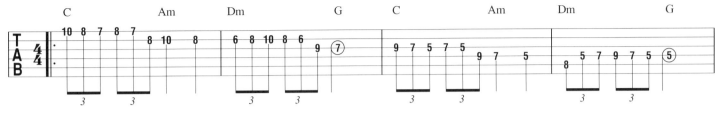

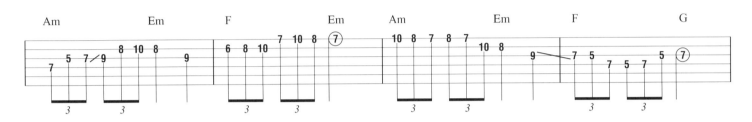

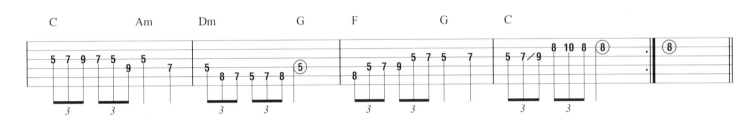

Solo 34: A/F#m

Track 250 Backing Track 387

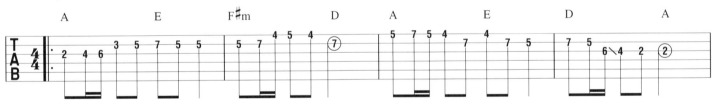

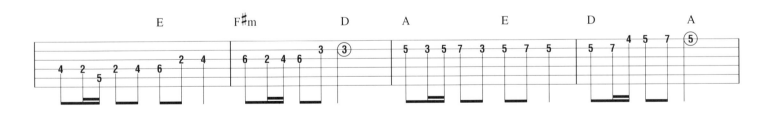

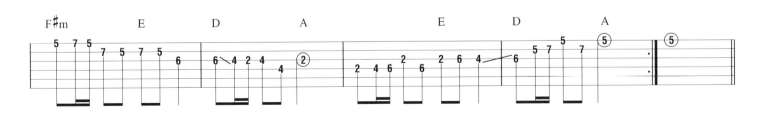

106

Solo 35: E/C#m

Track 251   Backing Track 393

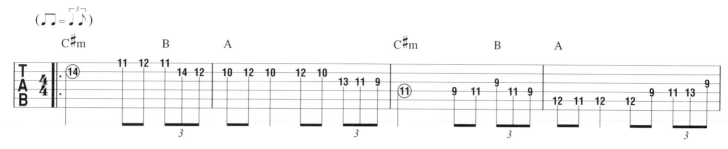

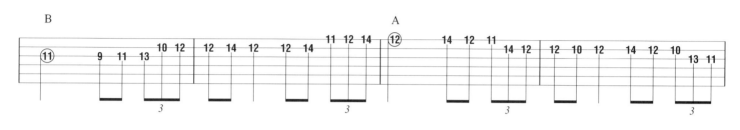

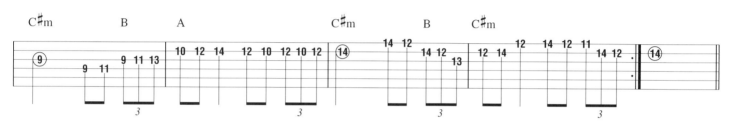

Solo 36: D/Bm

Track 252   Backing Track 388

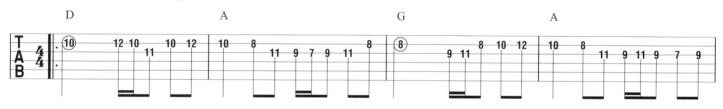

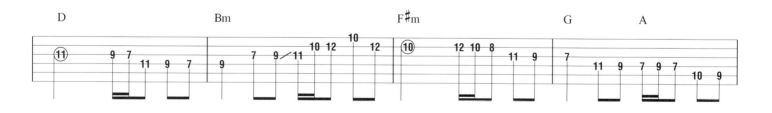

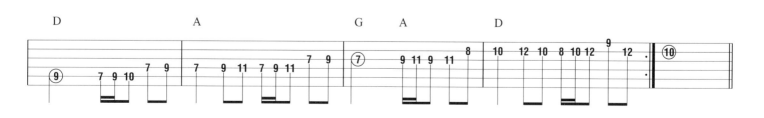

Chapter 11: Sixth-String-Root Upper-Diagonal Dorian Scales with Three-Notes-Per-String Fingerings

Let's continue our process of converting our one-position fingerings into three-notes-per-string fingerings by applying the concept to the upper portion of the Dorian scale. Our new fingering enables us to easily shift between the upper portion of Diagonal Pentatonic 1 and the Dorian "flavor notes." Continue using the black and white color coding to visualize the scale.

One-Position Fingering

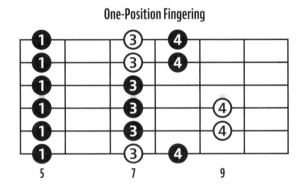

Upper-Diagonal Fingering

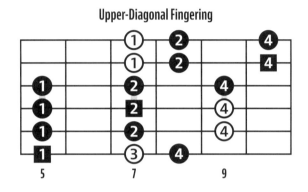

One-Position Intervals

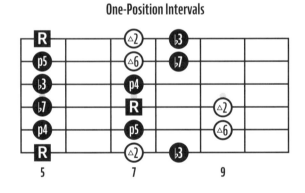

Upper-Diagonal Intervals

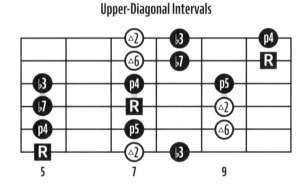

Try applying rhythms to the exercises below and pay attention to the fingerings as you work through them.

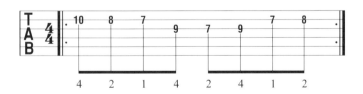

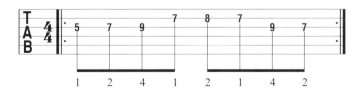

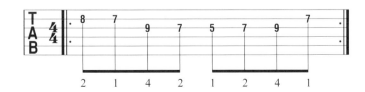

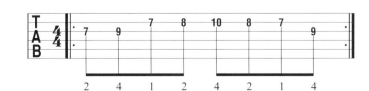

Descending Cells in G Dorian

Play the cell as written, then move it to the new tonal center using the indicated fret number as your guide. Apply a rhythm from below or from the Appendix. Use the scale diagrams and corresponding audio track to change keys. Continue playing the rhythm and improvise your note choices using these backing tracks: G Blues Backing Track 400 for Rhythm 1, C Dorian Backing Track 408 for Rhythm 2, A Blues Backing Track 403 for Rhythm 3, and E Dorian Backing Track 409 for Rhythm 4.

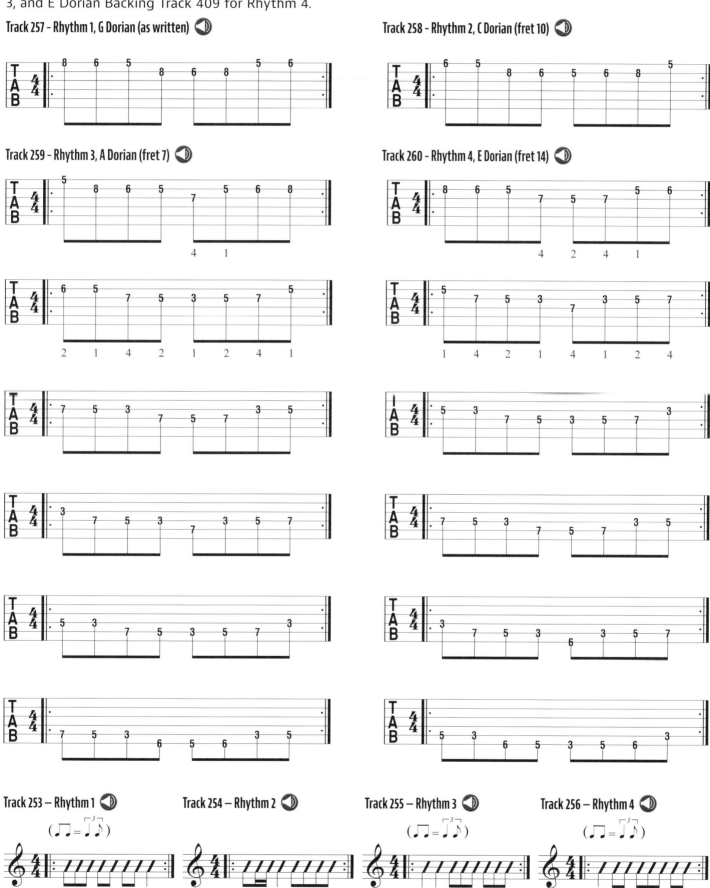

Track 257 - Rhythm 1, G Dorian (as written)

Track 258 - Rhythm 2, C Dorian (fret 10)

Track 259 - Rhythm 3, A Dorian (fret 7)

Track 260 - Rhythm 4, E Dorian (fret 14)

Track 253 – Rhythm 1

Track 254 – Rhythm 2

Track 255 – Rhythm 3

Track 256 – Rhythm 4

Ascending Cells in C Dorian

Play the cell as written, then move it to the new tonal center using the indicated fret number as your guide. Apply a rhythm from below or from the Appendix. Use the scale diagrams and corresponding audio track to change keys. Continue playing the rhythm and improvise your note choices using these backing tracks: G Blues Backing Track 400 for Rhythm 1, C Dorian Backing Track 408 for Rhythm 2, A Blues Backing Track 403 for Rhythm 3, and E Dorian Backing Track 409 for Rhythm 4.

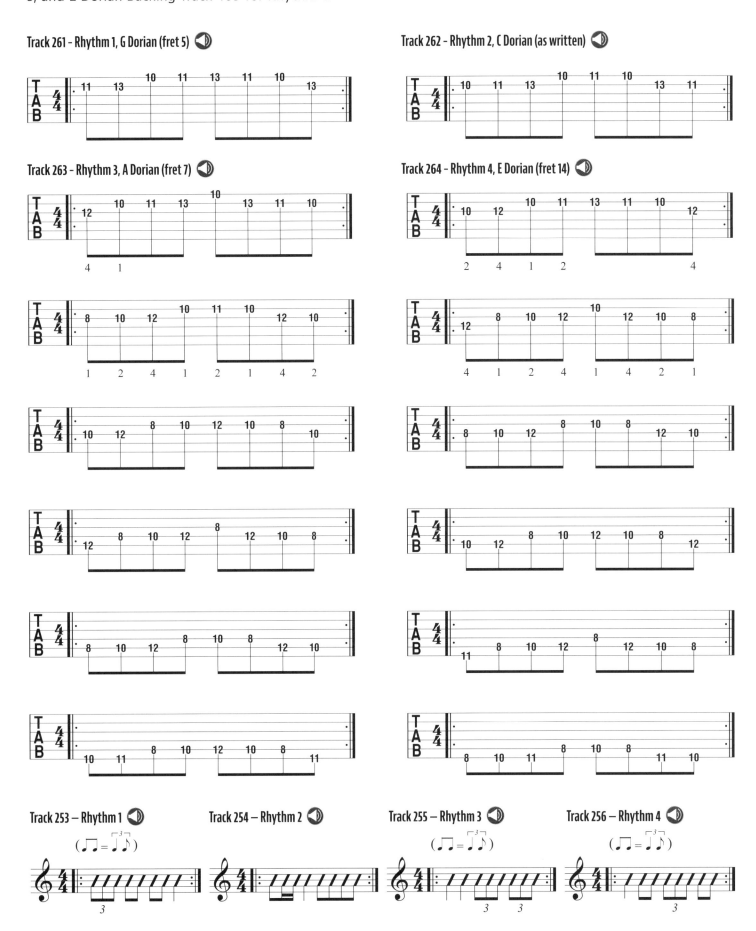

Descending Cells Connected in A Dorian

Track 265 - Rhythm 3

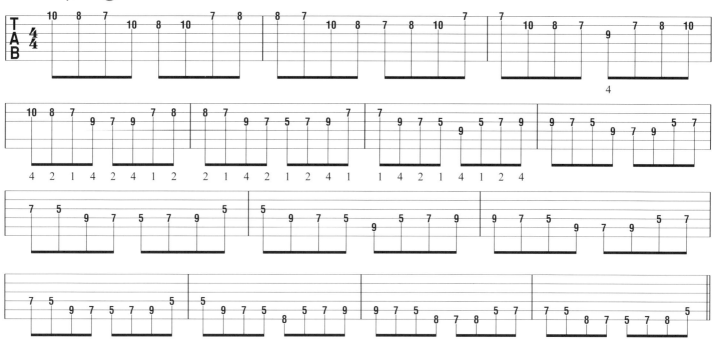

Ascending Cells Connected in E Dorian

Track 266 - Rhythm 4

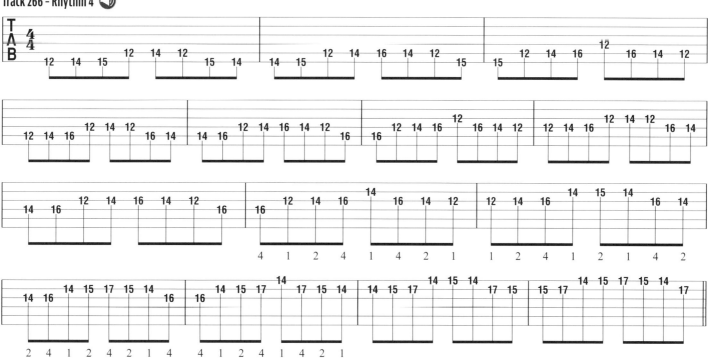

When you can play these easily, take the guide away and use: G Blues Backing Track 400 for Rhythm 1, C Dorian Backing Track 408 for Rhythm 2, A Blues Backing Track 403 for Rhythm 3, and E Dorian Backing Track 409 for Rhythm 4. More rhythms can be found in the Appendix.

Solo 37: G Dorian

Track 267  Backing Track 400

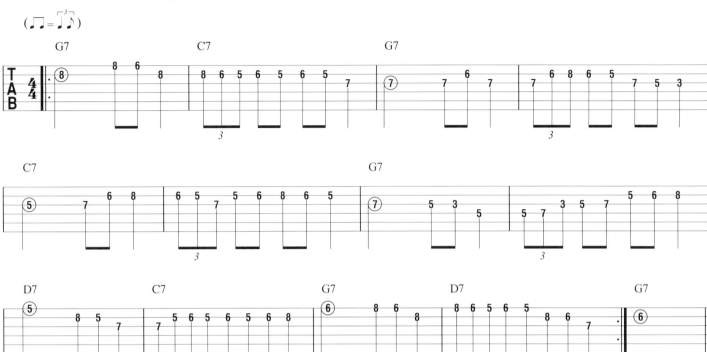

Solo 38: C Dorian

Track 268 Backing Track 408

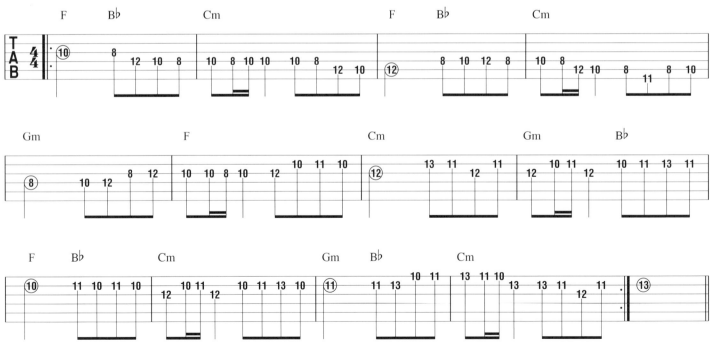

Solo 39: A Dorian

Track 269 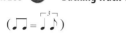 Backing Track 403

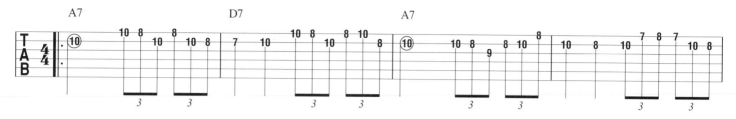

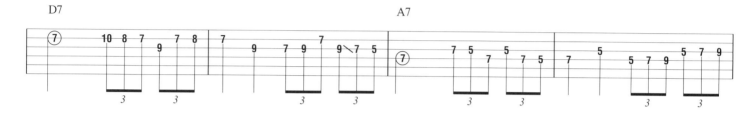

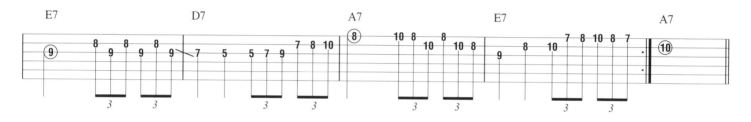

Solo 40: E Dorian

Track 270 Backing Track 409

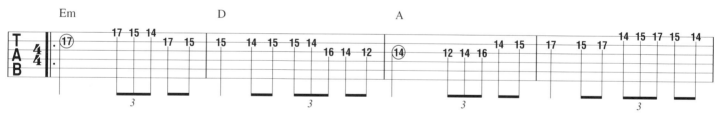

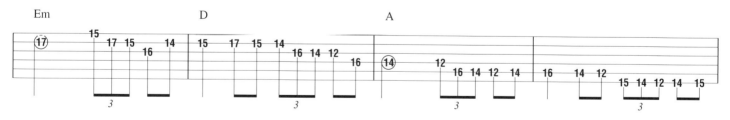

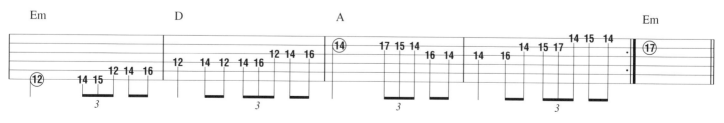

Chapter 12: Fifth-String-Root Major and Minor Scales with One-Position Fingerings

To develop the ability to add our new sounds in other areas of the fretboard, we will begin studying where our new scales intersect with Pentatonic Fingering 4, and the fifth-string-root chords that are contained within it. As before, an important part of the process is examining where the "flavor notes" shown in white are combined with the black dots from Pentatonic Fingering 4 you've already learned.

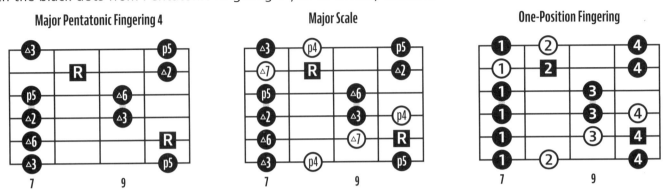

Play the following example to hear the major scale sound and visualize the chord within it.

Track 271

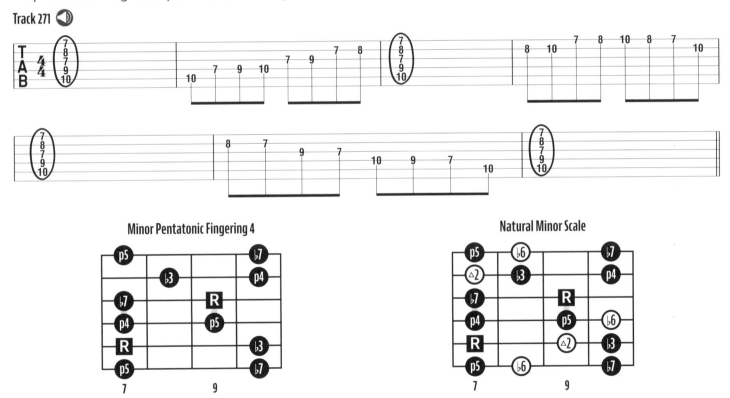

Play the following example to hear the natural minor scale sound and visualize the chord within it.

Track 272

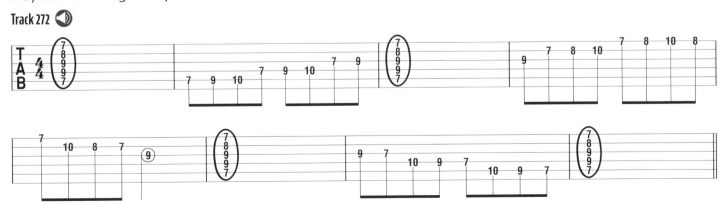

Descending Cells in the Key of G/Em

Play the cell as written, then move it to the new key using the indicated fret number as your guide. Apply a rhythm from below or from the Appendix. Use the scale diagrams and corresponding audio track to change keys. Continue playing the rhythm and improvise your note choices using these backing tracks: E Minor Backing Track 396 for Rhythm 1, E Backing Track 383 for Rhythm 2, B Minor Backing Track 398 for Rhythm 3, and F# Minor Backing Track 395 for Rhythm 4.

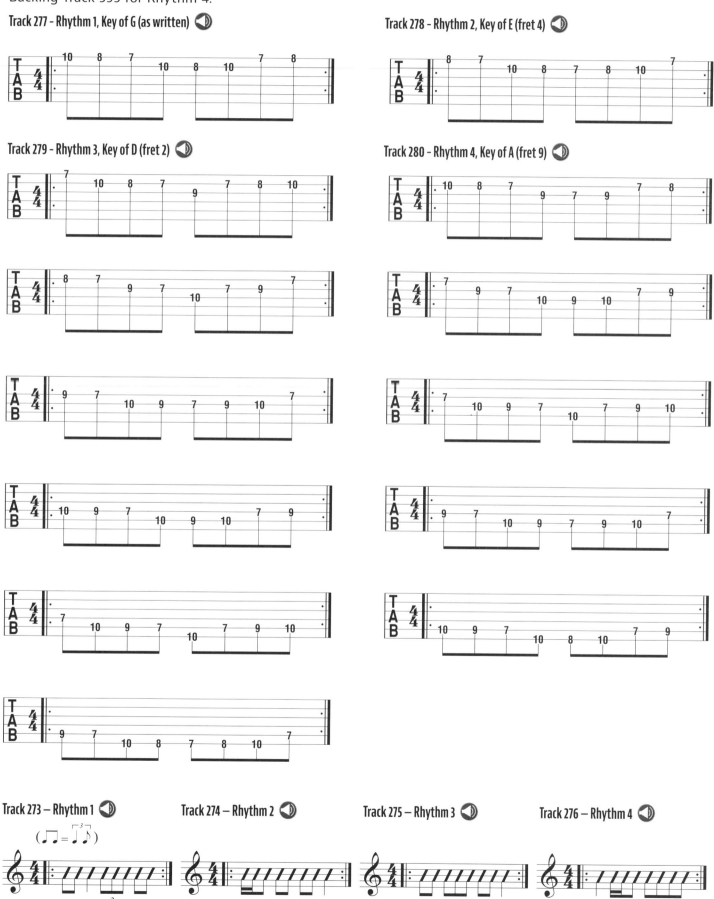

Ascending Cells in the Key of E/C♯m

Play the cell as written, then move it to the new key using the indicated fret number as your guide. Apply a rhythm from below or from the Appendix. Use the scale diagrams and corresponding audio track to change keys. Continue playing the rhythm and improvise your note choices using these backing tracks: E Minor Backing Track 396 for Rhythm 1, E Backing Track 383 for Rhythm 2, B Minor Backing Track 398 for Rhythm 3, and F♯ Minor Backing Track 395 for Rhythm 4.

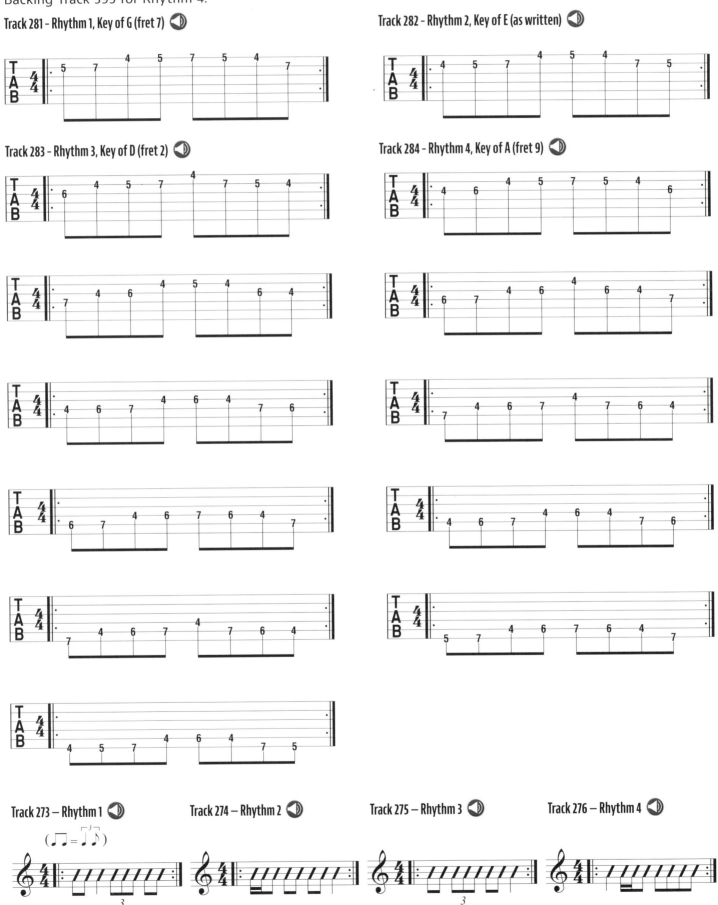

Track 281 - Rhythm 1, Key of G (fret 7)

Track 282 - Rhythm 2, Key of E (as written)

Track 283 - Rhythm 3, Key of D (fret 2)

Track 284 - Rhythm 4, Key of A (fret 9)

Track 273 – Rhythm 1   Track 274 – Rhythm 2   Track 275 – Rhythm 3   Track 276 – Rhythm 4

Descending Cells Connected in the Key of D/Bm

Track 285 – Rhythm 3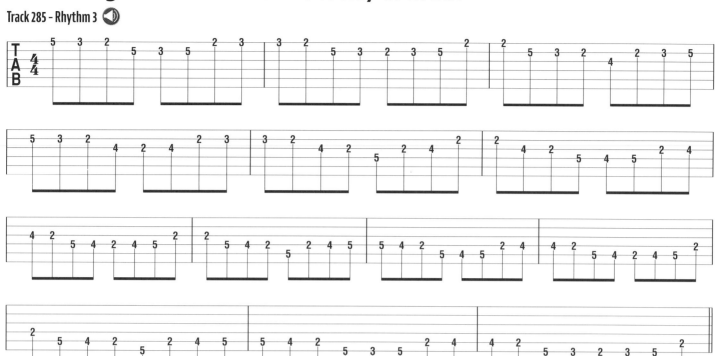

Ascending Cells Connected in the Key of A/F♯m

Track 286 – Rhythm 4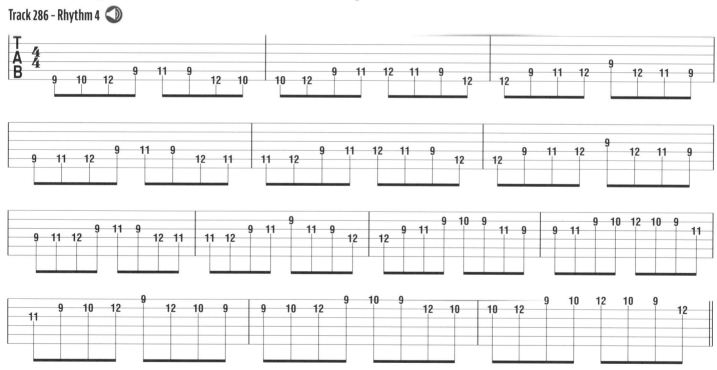

When you can play these easily, take the guide away and use: E Minor Backing Track 396 for Rhythm 1, E Backing Track 383 for Rhythm 2, B Minor Backing Track 398 for Rhythm 3, and F♯ Minor Backing Track 395 for Rhythm 4. More rhythms can be found in the Appendix.

Track 273 – Rhythm 1   Track 274 – Rhythm 2   Track 275 – Rhythm 3   Track 276 – Rhythm 4

Solo 41: G/Em

Track 287 Backing Track 396

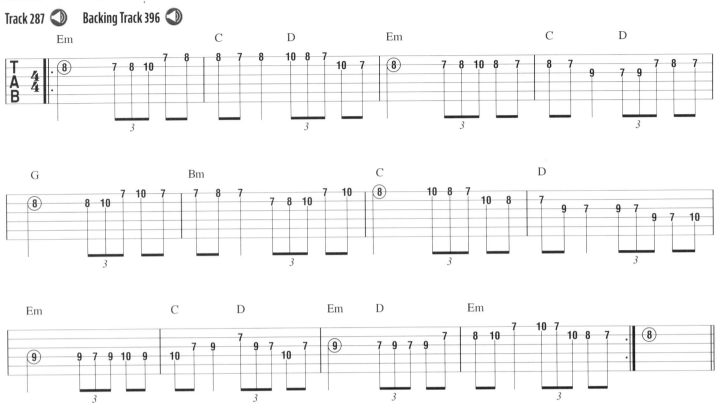

Solo 42: E/C#m

Track 288 Backing Track 383

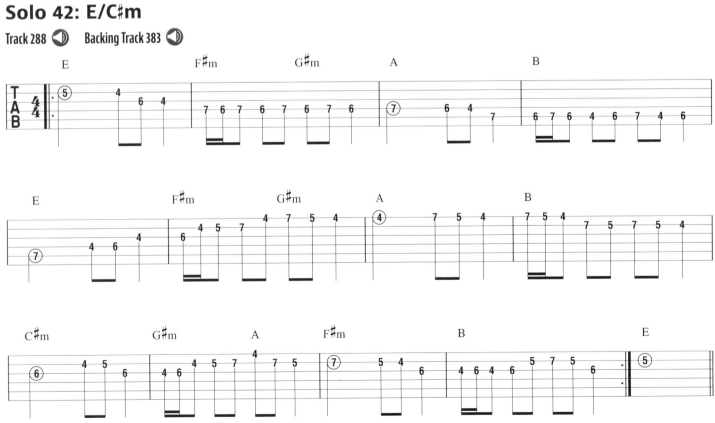

Solo 43: D/Bm

Track 289 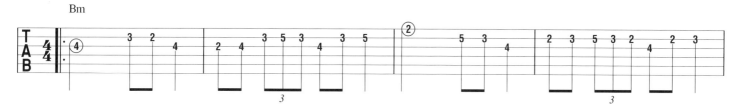 Backing Track 398

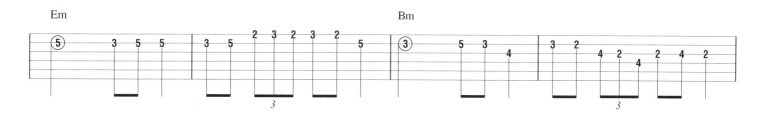

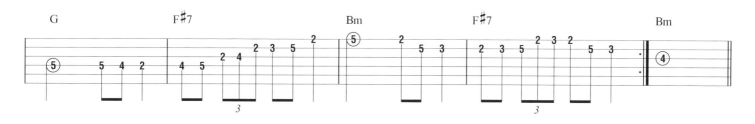

Solo 44: A/F#m

Track 290 Backing Track 395

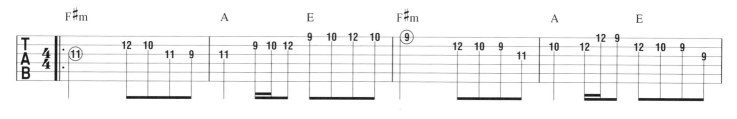

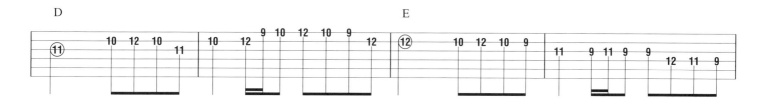

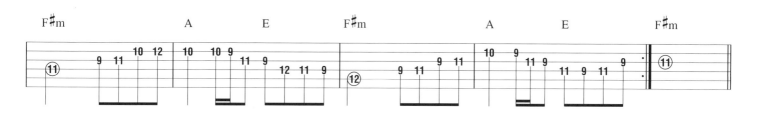

Chapter 13: Fifth-String-Root Dorian Scales with One-Position Fingerings

As we explore adding the Dorian sound to Pentatonic Fingering 4, you will notice that the fingering is identical to the major and natural minor scales with their roots on the sixth string. Fingerings will repeat themselves due to the fact that they are modes of the major scale. A music theory book will shed light on this matter. Since you already know the fingering from Chapter 6, the new goal is to make it sound like Dorian by changing its starting or root note to the fifth and third strings. These new root locations are indicated by the squares in the diagrams below. Notice how the other intervals now relate to the new root notes.

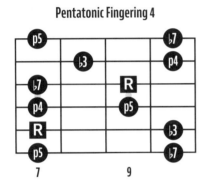

Pentatonic Fingering 4

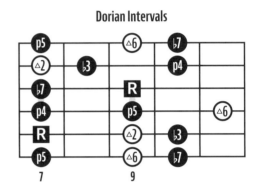

Dorian Intervals

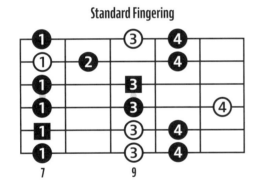

Standard Fingering

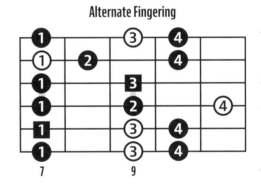

Alternate Fingering

Play the following example to hear the brighter Dorian scale sound and visualize the chord within it.

Track 291

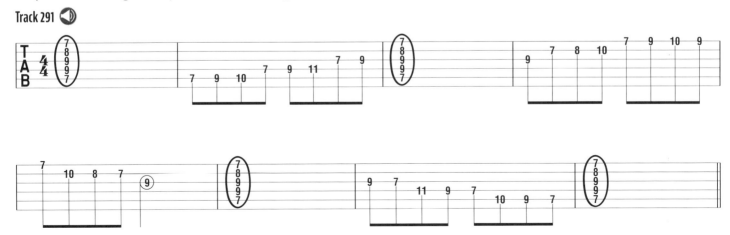

Descending Cells in E Dorian

Play the cell as written, then move it to the new tonal center using the indicated fret number as your guide. Apply a rhythm from below or from the Appendix. Use the scale diagrams and corresponding audio track to change keys. Continue playing the rhythm and improvise your note choices using these backing tracks: E Blues Backing Track 401 for Rhythm 1, G Dorian Backing Track 410 for Rhythm 2, C Dorian Backing Track 406 for Rhythm 3, and D Blues Backing Track 402 for Rhythm 4.

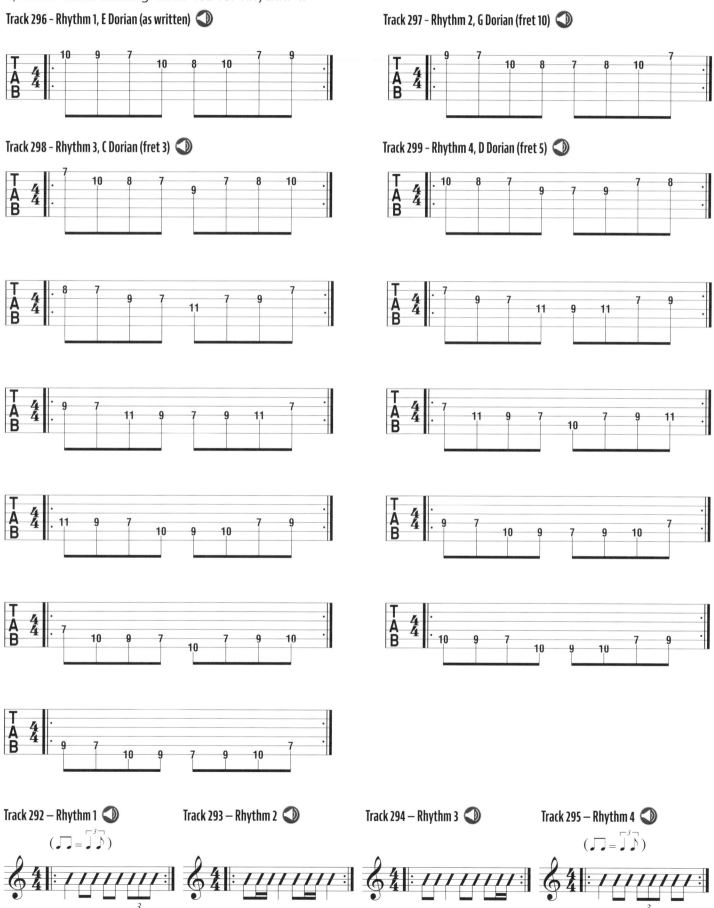

Track 296 - Rhythm 1, E Dorian (as written)

Track 297 - Rhythm 2, G Dorian (fret 10)

Track 298 - Rhythm 3, C Dorian (fret 3)

Track 299 - Rhythm 4, D Dorian (fret 5)

Track 292 – Rhythm 1 **Track 293 – Rhythm 2** **Track 294 – Rhythm 3** **Track 295 – Rhythm 4**

Ascending Cells in G Dorian

Play the cell as written, then move it to the new tonal center using the indicated fret number as your guide. Apply a rhythm from below or from the Appendix. Use the scale diagrams and corresponding audio track to change keys. Continue playing the rhythm and improvise your note choices using these backing tracks: E Blues Backing Track 401 for Rhythm 1, G Dorian Backing Track 410 for Rhythm 2, C Dorian Backing Track 406 for Rhythm 3, and D Blues Backing Track 402 for Rhythm 4.

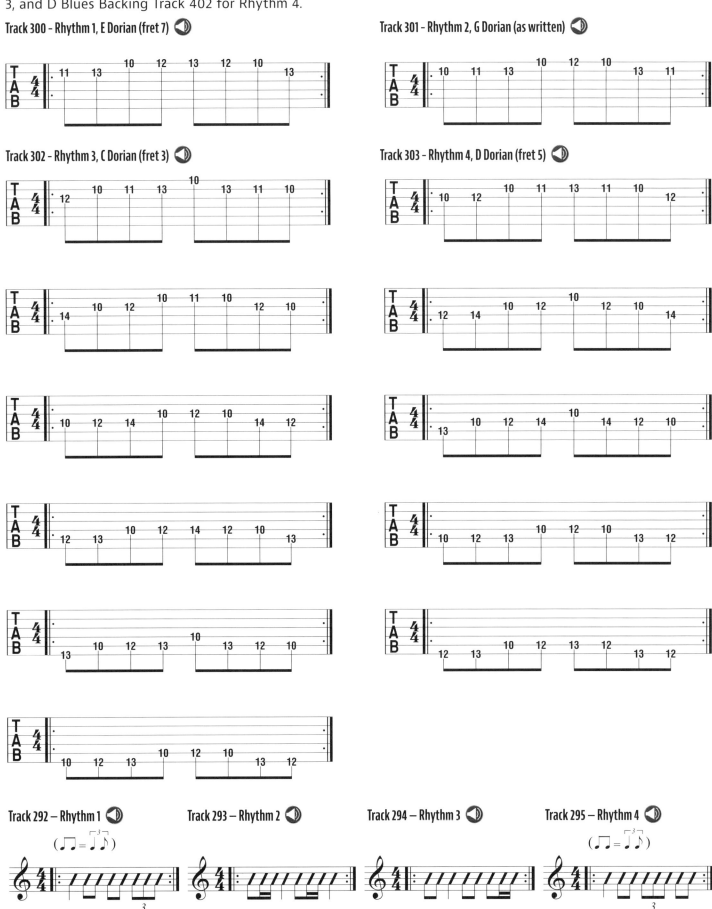

Descending Cells Connected in C Dorian

Track 304 – Rhythm 3

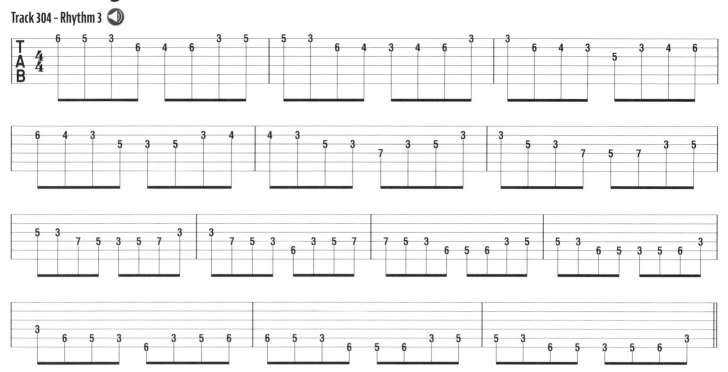

Ascending Cells Connected in D Dorian

Track 305 – Rhythm 4

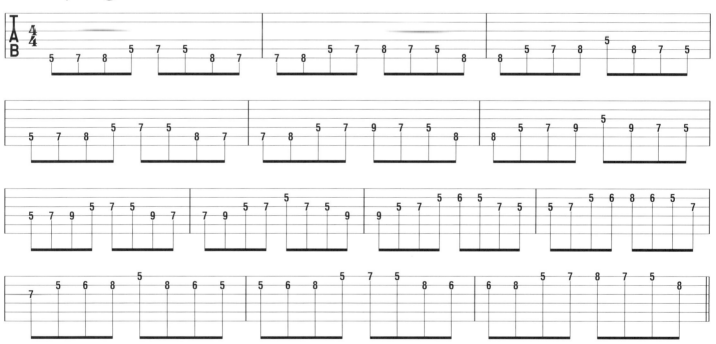

When you can play these easily, take the guide away and use: E Blues Backing Track 401 for Rhythm 1, G Dorian Backing Track 410 for Rhythm 2, C Dorian Backing Track 406 for Rhythm 3, and D Blues Backing Track 402 for Rhythm 4. More rhythms can be found in the Appendix.

Track 292 – Rhythm 1   Track 293 – Rhythm 2   Track 294 – Rhythm 3   Track 295 – Rhythm 4

Solo 45: E Dorian

Track 306   Backing Track 401

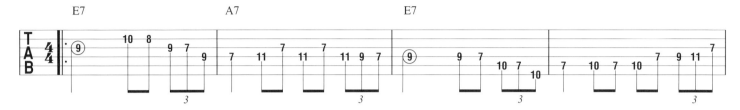

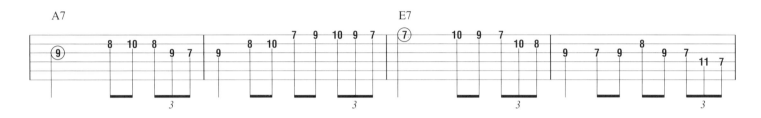

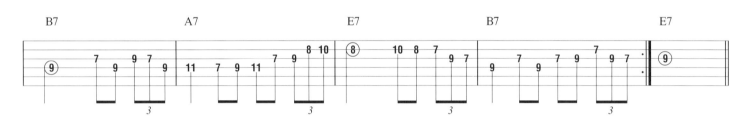

Solo 46: G Dorian

Track 307   Backing Track 410

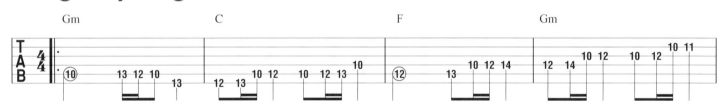

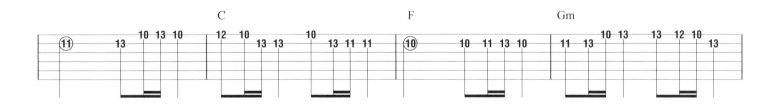

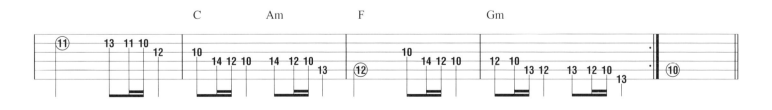

Solo 47: C Dorian

Track 308 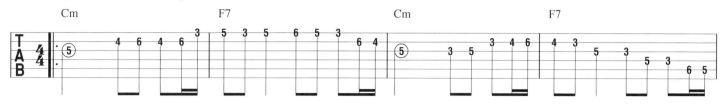 Backing Track 406

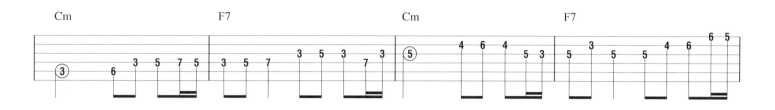

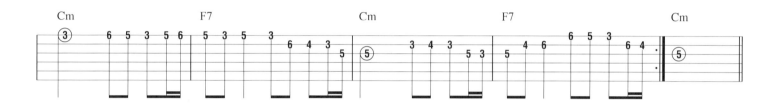

Solo 48: D Dorian

Track 309 Backing Track 402

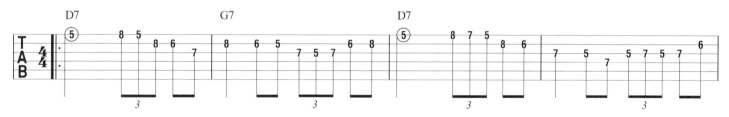

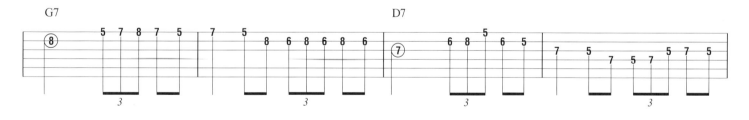

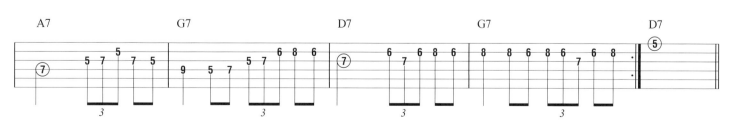

Chapter 14: Fifth-String-Root Lower-Diagonal Major and Minor Scales with Three-Notes-Per-String Fingerings

It is a great advantage to have the ability to keep three notes per string when working in the Pentatonic Fingering 4 area around the fifth-string-root chords. As you practice these fingerings, you'll realize that you have been here before. They are literally identical to the fingerings in Chapter 11. Our task is to repurpose the scale fingerings and learn how they sound in their new context. Try playing the black dots to hear the familiar sound of Pentatonic Fingering 4, then add the white dots to hear the added scale flavors. Take note of where the fingerings overlap with the lower portion of Diagonal Pentatonic Fingering 4.

One-Position Fingering

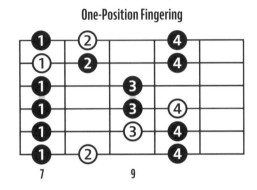

Lower-Diagonal Fingering

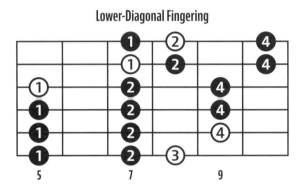

Major Intervals

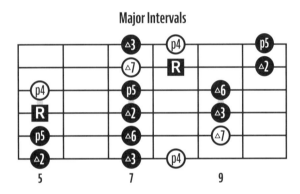

Minor Intervals

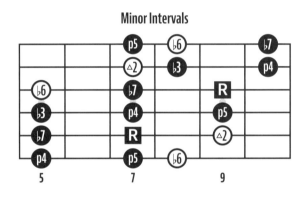

As you play the following exercises, observe the extra emphasis on the root note. It's the first step to hearing the sound of the scale.

G Major Scale

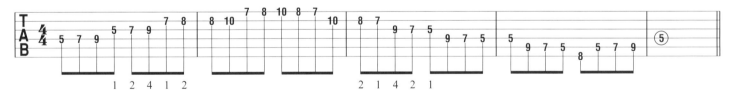

E Natural Minor Scale

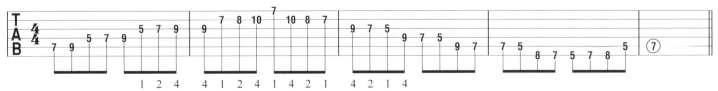

Descending Cells in the Key of G/Em

Play the cell as written, then move it to the new key using the indicated fret number as your guide. Apply a rhythm from below or from the Appendix. Use the scale diagrams and corresponding audio track to change keys. Continue playing the rhythm and improvise your note choices using these backing tracks: E Blues Backing Track 401 for Rhythm 1, G Dorian Backing Track 410 for Rhythm 2, C Dorian Backing Track 406 for Rhythm 3, and D Blues Backing Track 402 for Rhythm 4.

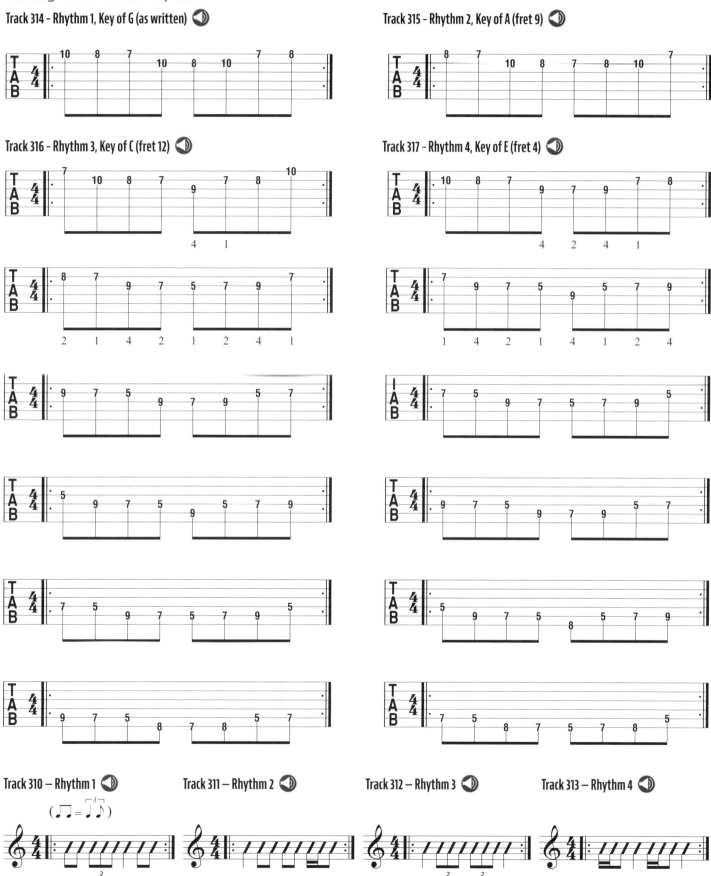

Track 314 – Rhythm 1, Key of G (as written)

Track 315 – Rhythm 2, Key of A (fret 9)

Track 316 – Rhythm 3, Key of C (fret 12)

Track 317 – Rhythm 4, Key of E (fret 4)

Track 310 – Rhythm 1 **Track 311 – Rhythm 2** **Track 312 – Rhythm 3** **Track 313 – Rhythm 4**

Ascending Cells in the Key of A/F♯m

Play the cell as written, then move it to the new key using the indicated fret number as your guide. Apply a rhythm from below or from the Appendix. Use the scale diagrams and corresponding audio track to change keys. Continue playing the rhythm and improvise your note choices using these backing tracks: G Backing Track 391 for Rhythm 1, F♯ Minor Backing Track 394 for Rhythm 2, C Backing Track 382 for Rhythm 3, and E Backing Track 385 for Rhythm 4.

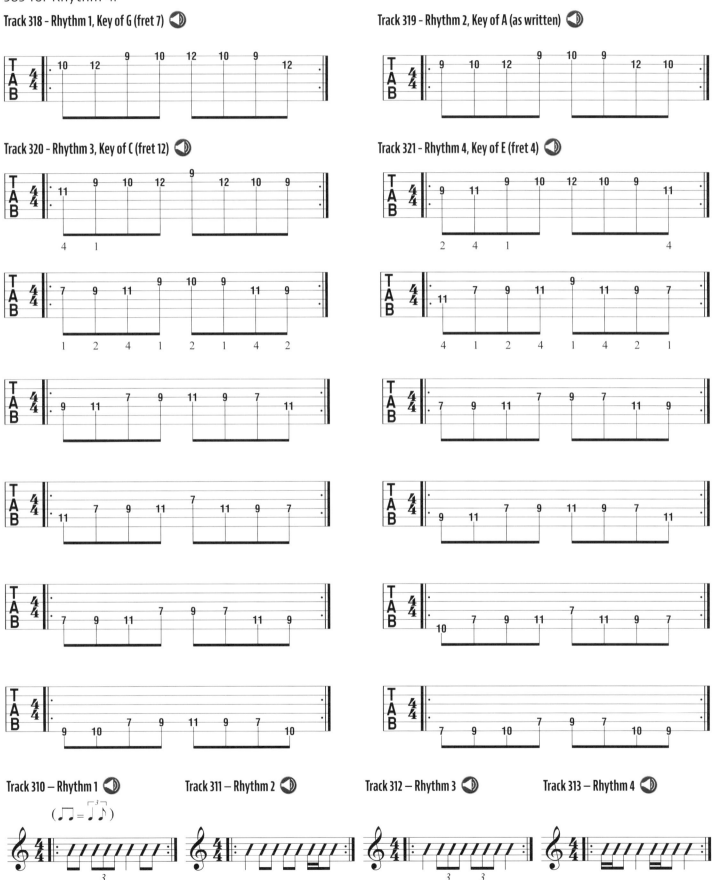

Descending Cells Connected in the Key of C/Am

Track 322 - Rhythm 3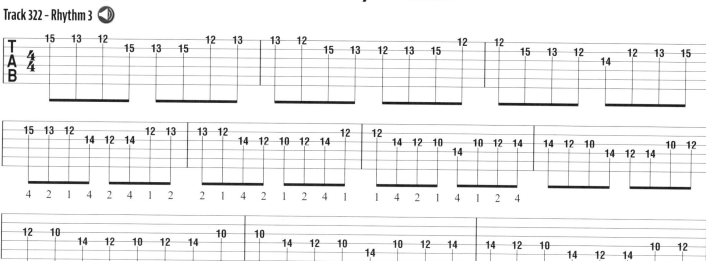

Ascending Cells Connected in the Key of E/C♯m

Track 323 - Rhythm 4

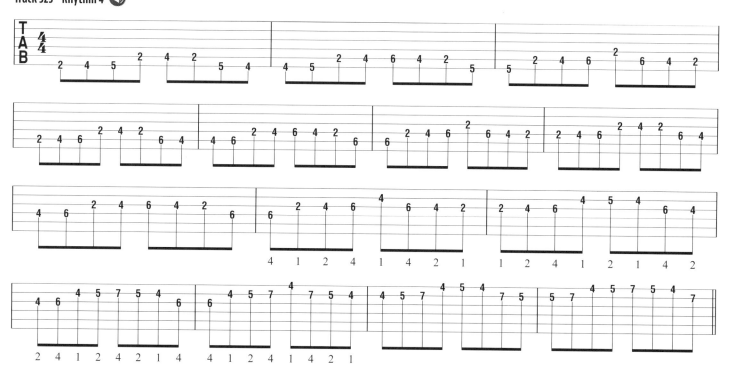

When you can play these easily, take the guide away and use: G Backing Track 391 for Rhythm 1, F♯ Minor Backing Track 394 for Rhythm 2, C Backing Track 382 for Rhythm 3, and E Backing Track 385 for Rhythm 4. More rhythms can be found in the Appendix.

Track 310 – Rhythm 1   Track 311 – Rhythm 2   Track 312 – Rhythm 3   Track 313 – Rhythm 4

Solo 49: G/Em

Track 324 Backing Track 391

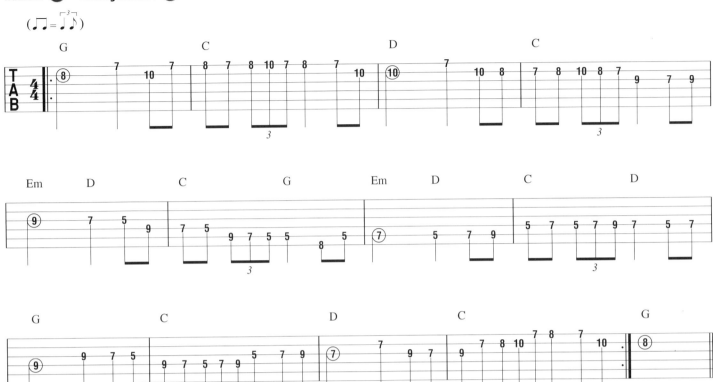

Solo 50: A/F#m

Track 325 Backing Track 394

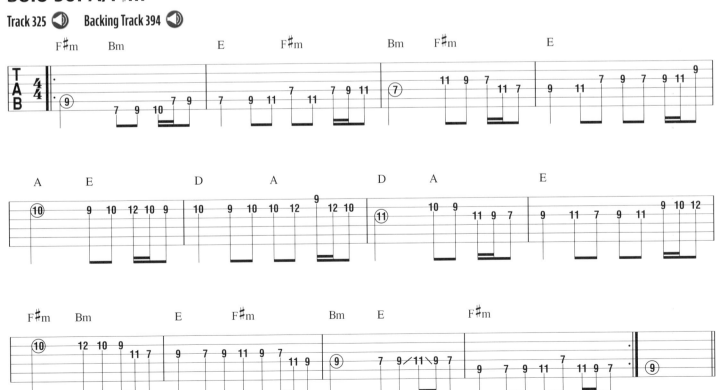

Solo 51: C/Am

Track 326 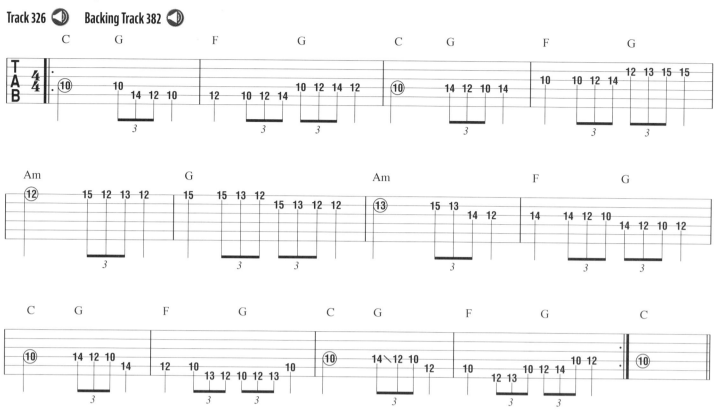 Backing Track 382

Solo 52: E/C#m

Track 327 Backing Track 385

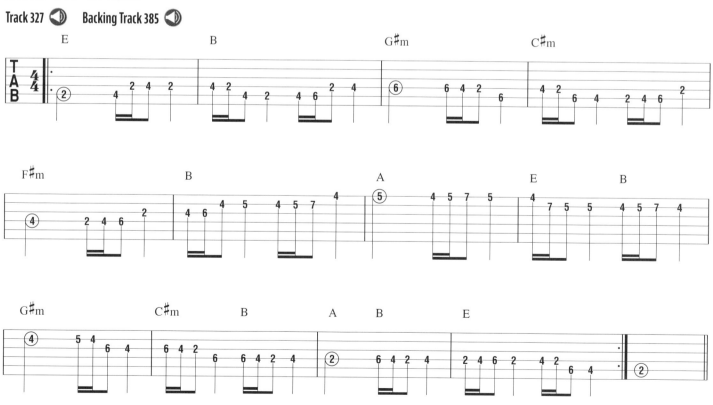

Chapter 15: Fifth-String-Root Lower-Diagonal Dorian Scales with Three-Notes-Per-String Fingerings

As we apply the concept of shifting positions to keep three notes per string for the Dorian scale, you will quickly discover that the fingerings are identical to those of Chapter 8. Our job is to repurpose the fingering we've already learned and use it in a Dorian context. A great way to start is to play the pentatonic black dots in the following diagrams before adding the white "flavor notes." Try starting and ending on the roots to emphasize the sound of the scale.

One-Position Fingering

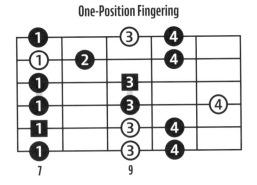

Lower-Diagonal Fingering

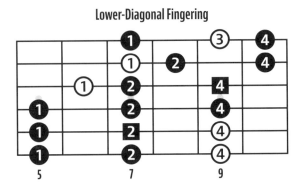

One-Position Intervals

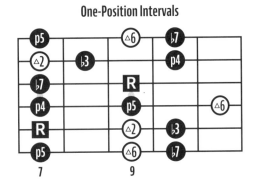

Lower-Diagonal Intervals

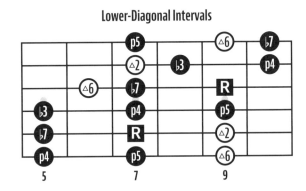

Emphasizing the roots in the following exercise will help you hear the sound of the scale.

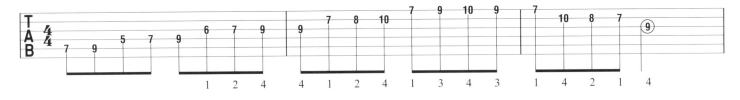

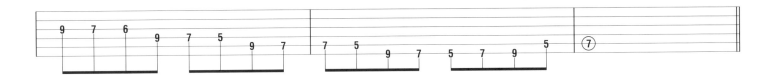

Descending Cells in E Dorian

Play the cell as written, then move it to the new tonal center using the indicated fret number as your guide. Apply a rhythm from below or from the Appendix. Use the scale diagrams and corresponding audio track to change keys. Continue playing the rhythm and improvise your note choices using these backing tracks: E Blues Backing Track 401 for Rhythm 1, G Dorian Backing Track 410 for Rhythm 2, A Blues Backing Track 403 for Rhythm 3, and D Dorian Backing Track 407 for Rhythm 4.

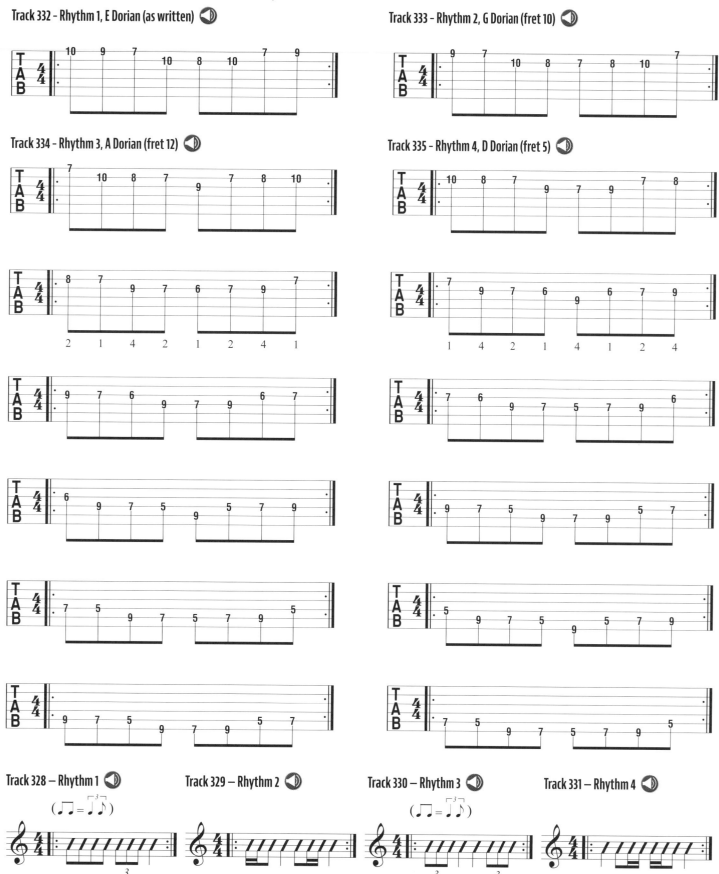

Track 332 – Rhythm 1, E Dorian (as written)

Track 333 – Rhythm 2, G Dorian (fret 10)

Track 334 – Rhythm 3, A Dorian (fret 12)

Track 335 – Rhythm 4, D Dorian (fret 5)

Track 328 – Rhythm 1   Track 329 – Rhythm 2   Track 330 – Rhythm 3   Track 331 – Rhythm 4

Ascending Cells in G Dorian

Play the cell as written, then move it to the new tonal center using the indicated fret number as your guide. Apply a rhythm from below or from the Appendix. Use the scale diagrams and corresponding audio track to change keys. Continue playing the rhythm and improvise your note choices using these backing tracks: E Blues Backing Track 401 for Rhythm 1, G Dorian Backing Track 410 for Rhythm 2, A Blues Backing Track 403 for Rhythm 3, and D Dorian Backing Track 407 for Rhythm 4.

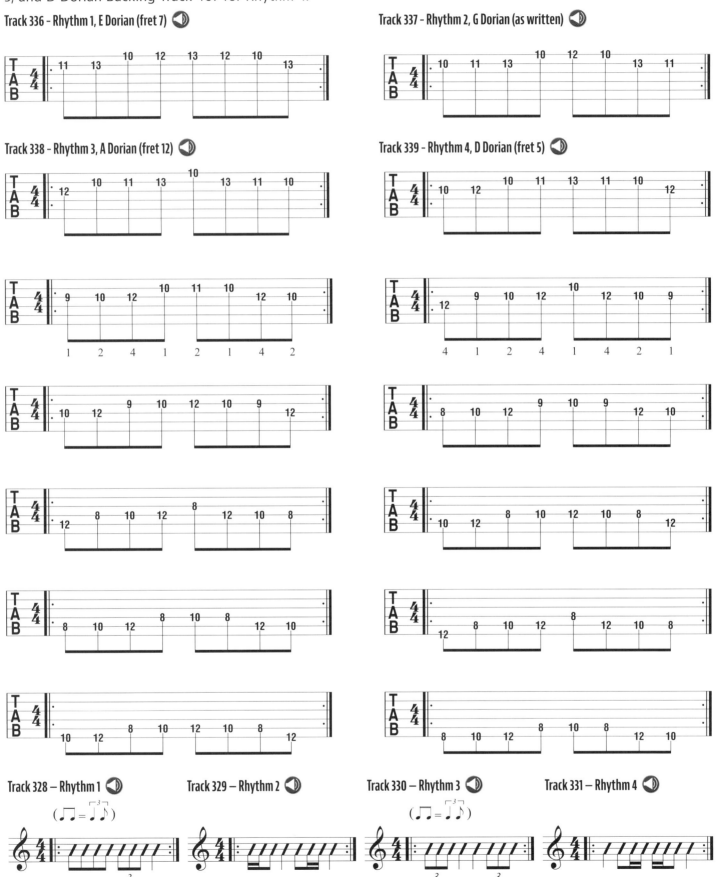

Track 336 - Rhythm 1, E Dorian (fret 7)

Track 337 - Rhythm 2, G Dorian (as written)

Track 338 - Rhythm 3, A Dorian (fret 12)

Track 339 - Rhythm 4, D Dorian (fret 5)

Track 328 – Rhythm 1   **Track 329 – Rhythm 2**   **Track 330 – Rhythm 3**   **Track 331 – Rhythm 4**

Descending Cells Connected in A Dorian

Track 340 - Rhythm 3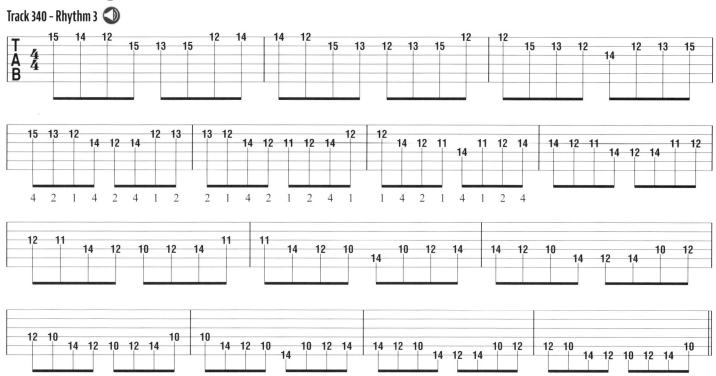

Ascending Cells Connected in D Dorian

Track 341 - Rhythm 4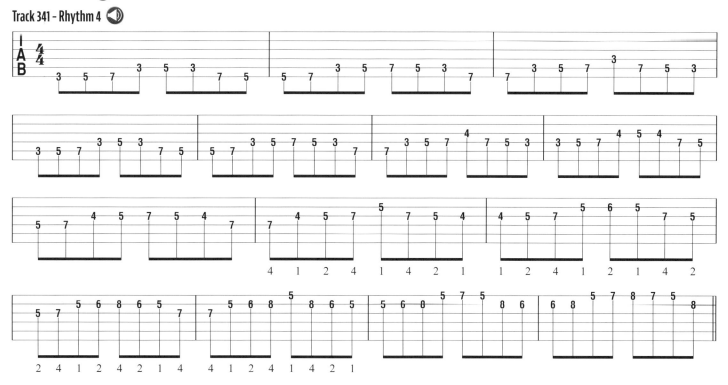

When you can play these easily, take the guide away and use: E Blues Backing Track 401 for Rhythm 1, G Dorian Backing Track 410 for Rhythm 2, A Blues Backing Track 403 for Rhythm 3, and D Dorian Backing Track 407 for Rhythm 4. More rhythms can be found in the Appendix.

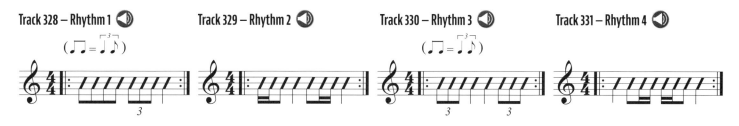

Track 328 – Rhythm 1   Track 329 – Rhythm 2   Track 330 – Rhythm 3   Track 331 – Rhythm 4

Solo 53: E Dorian

Track 342  Backing Track 401

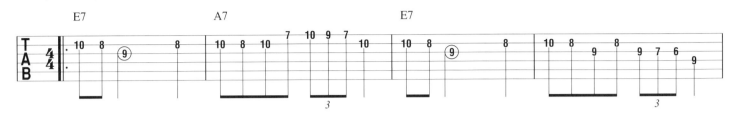

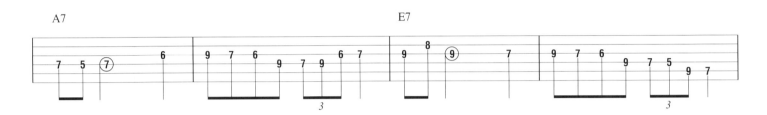

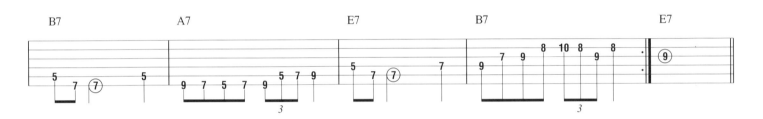

Solo 54: G Dorian

Track 343 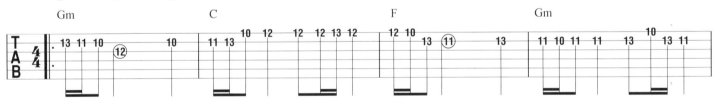 Backing Track 410

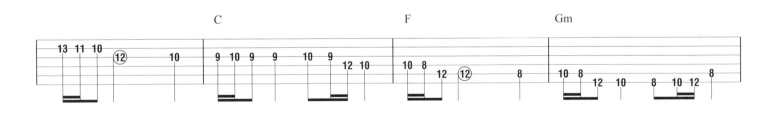

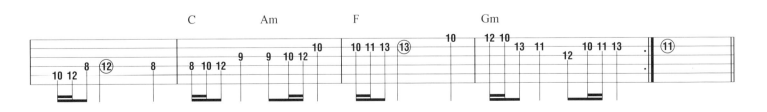

Solo 55: Am Dorian

Track 344  Backing Track 403

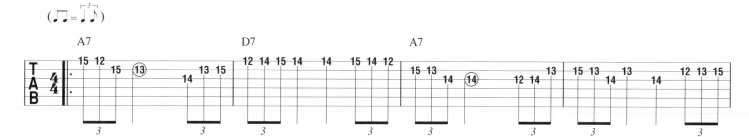

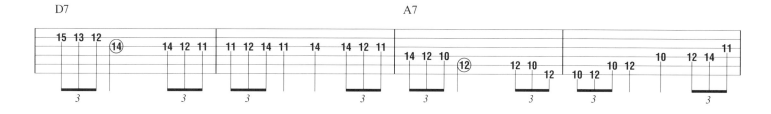

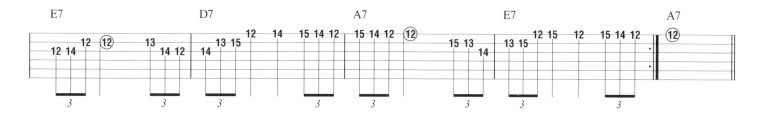

Solo 56: D Dorian

Track 345 Backing Track 407

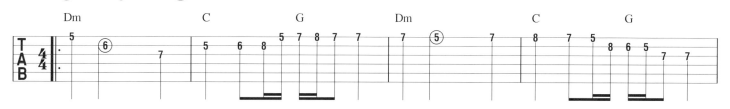

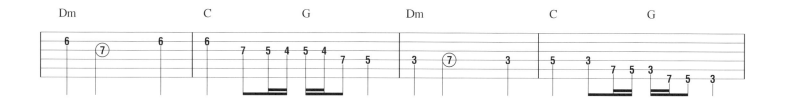

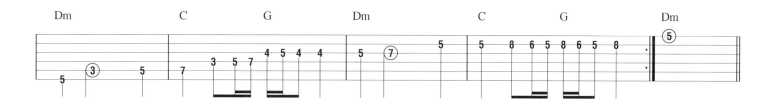

Chapter 16: Fifth-String-Root Upper-Diagonal Major and Minor Scales with Three-Notes-Per-String Fingerings

Shifting upwards from our major/natural minor one-position fingering creates a new three-notes-per-string fingering that covers the upper portion of Diagonal Pentatonic Fingering 4. As you begin absorbing the new pattern, try using the black dots/white dots approach to help relate the patterns.

One-Position Fingering

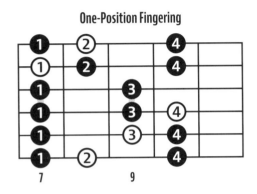

Upper-Diagonal Fingering

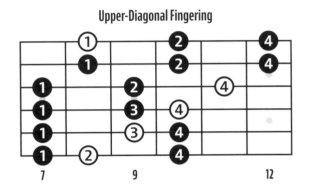

Major Intervals

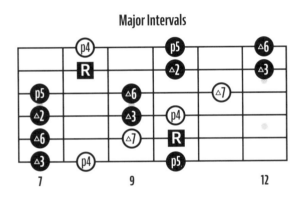

Minor Intervals

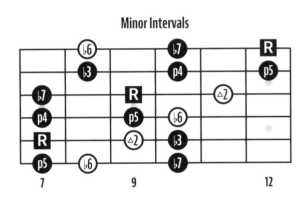

Practice the following exercises to get used to the new fingerings needed for shifting positions. Notice how the patterns impart the sound of each scale by starting from the root notes.

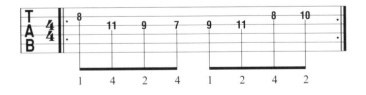

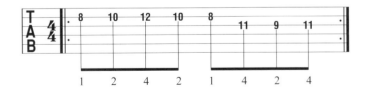

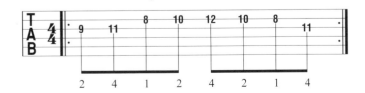

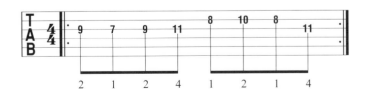

138

Descending Cells in the Key of D/Bm

Play the cell as written, then move it to the new key using the indicated fret number as your guide. Apply a rhythm from below or from the Appendix. Use the scale diagrams and corresponding audio track to change keys. Continue playing the rhythm and improvise your note choices using these backing tracks: D Backing Track 389 for Rhythm 1, A Backing Track 387 for Rhythm 2, E Minor Backing Track 396 for Rhythm 3, and C Backing Track 384 for Rhythm 4.

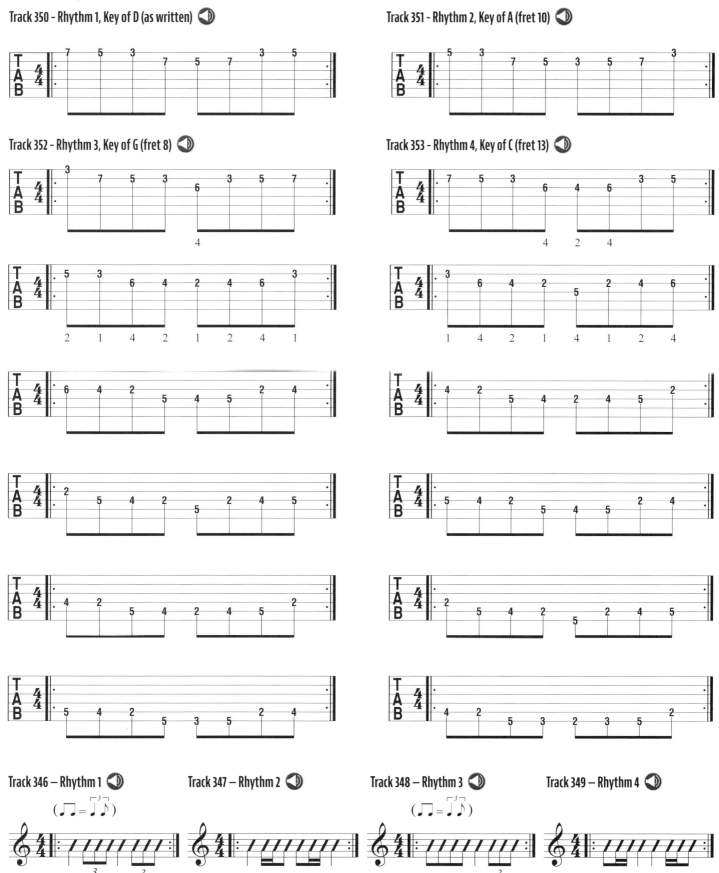

Ascending Cells in the Key of A/F♯m

Play the cell as written, then move it to the new key using the indicated fret number as your guide. Apply a rhythm from below or from the Appendix. Use the scale diagrams and corresponding audio track to change keys. Continue playing the rhythm and improvise your note choices using these backing tracks: D Backing Track 389 for Rhythm 1, A Backing Track 387 for Rhythm 2, E Minor Backing Track 396 for Rhythm 3, and C Backing Track 384 for Rhythm 4.

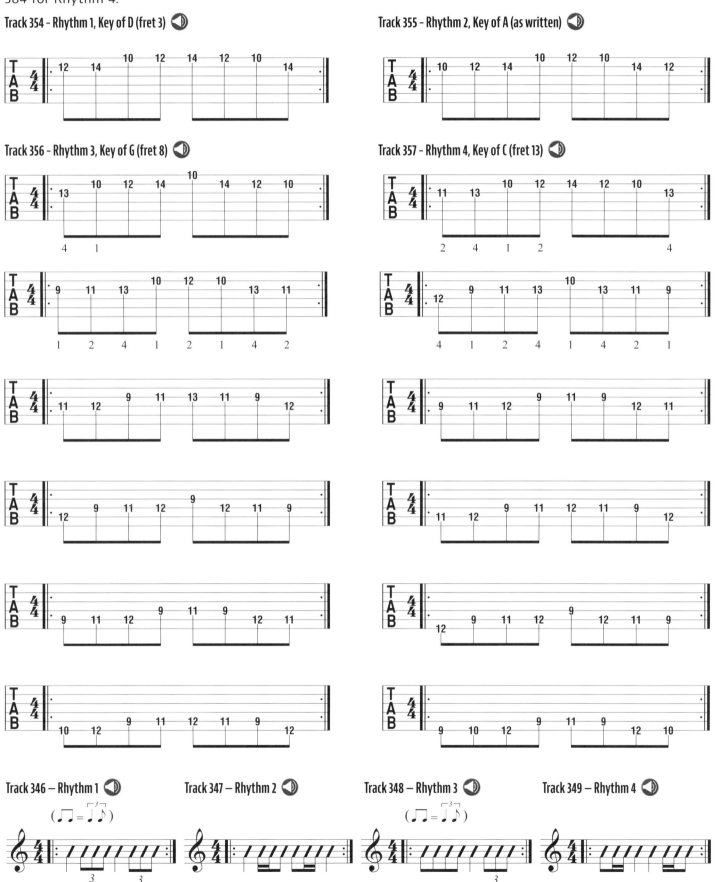

Track 354 – Rhythm 1, Key of D (fret 3)

Track 355 – Rhythm 2, Key of A (as written)

Track 356 – Rhythm 3, Key of G (fret 8)

Track 357 – Rhythm 4, Key of C (fret 13)

Track 346 – Rhythm 1   **Track 347 – Rhythm 2**   **Track 348 – Rhythm 3**   **Track 349 – Rhythm 4**

Descending Cells Connected in the Key of G/Em

Track 358 - Rhythm 3

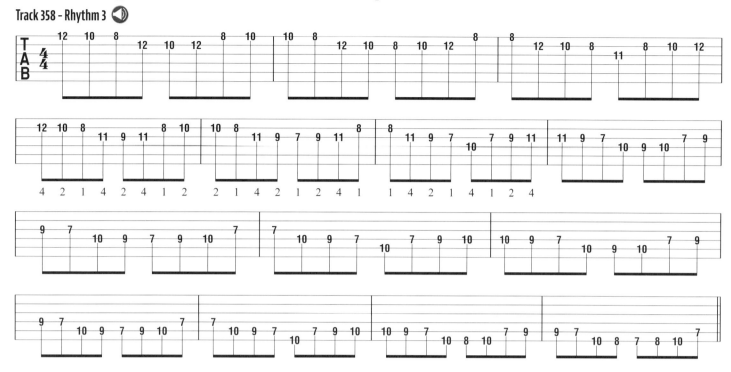

Ascending Cells Connected C/Am

Track 359 - Rhythm 4

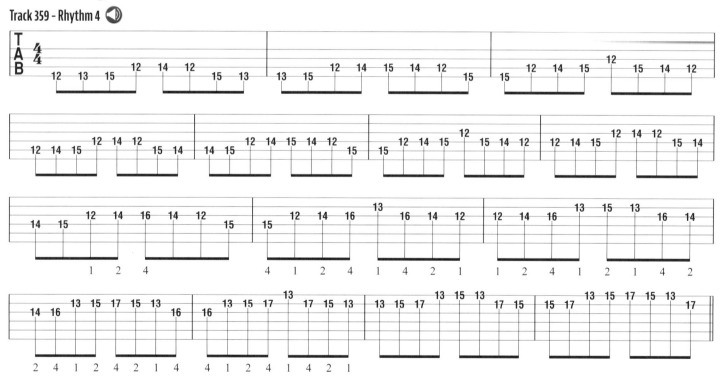

When you can play these easily, take the guide away and use: D Backing Track 389 for Rhythm 1, A Backing Track 387 for Rhythm 2, E Minor Backing Track 396 for Rhythm 3, and C Backing Track 384 for Rhythm 4. More rhythms can be found in the Appendix.

Track 346 – Rhythm 1   Track 347 – Rhythm 2   Track 348 – Rhythm 3   Track 349 – Rhythm 4

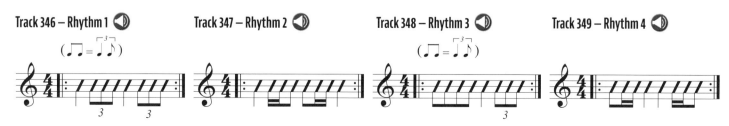

Solo 57: D/Bm

Track 360   Backing Track 389

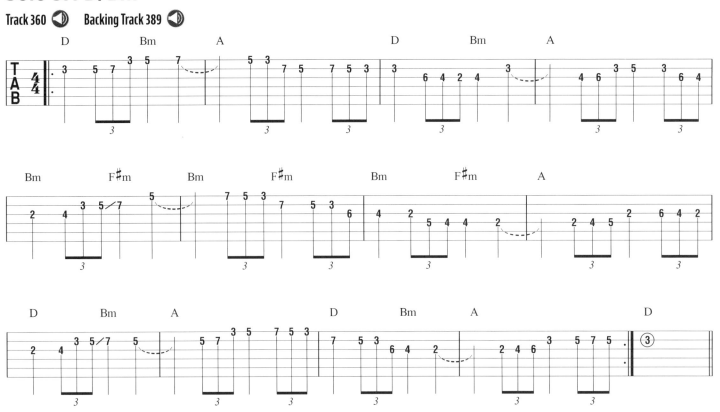

Solo 58: A/F#m

Track 361   Backing Track 387

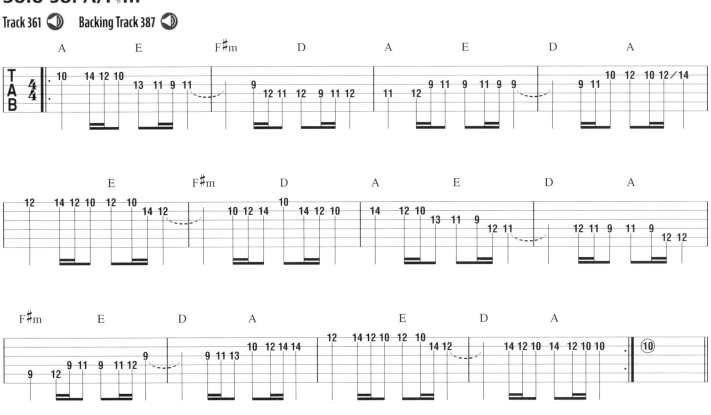

Solo 59: G/Em

Track 362 🔊 Backing Track 396 🔊

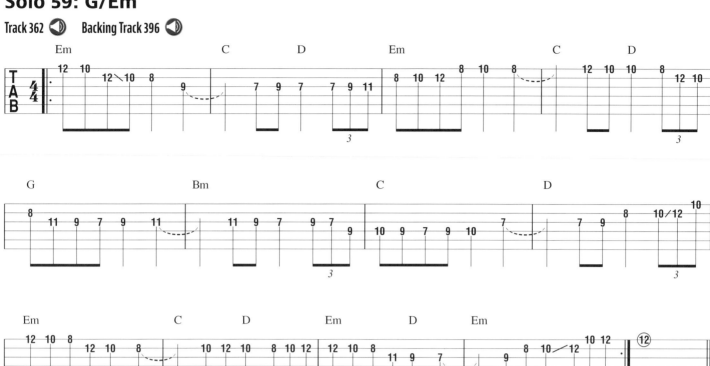

Solo 60: C/Am

Track 363 🔊 Backing Track 384 🔊

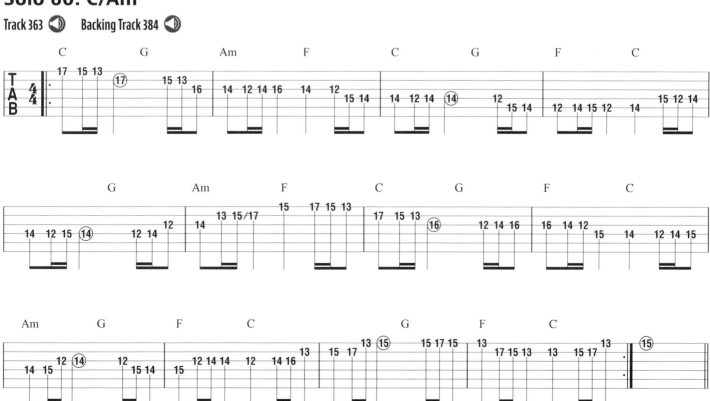

Chapter 17: Fifth-String-Root Upper-Diagonal Dorian Scales with Three-Notes-Per-String Fingerings

Congratulations on making it to the final fingering presented in this book! Upon completing this chapter, you will have developed the ability to mix the pentatonic scale with seven-note scales in the most used areas of the fretboard. As you shift up and out of the one-position Dorian scale you will notice the fingerings are identical to those in Chapter 10. Again it is a matter of reusing the fingering in a new context by emphasizing the roots. Mixing it with the familiar sound of the pentatonic by playing the black dots only can help you get a feel for the new context.

One-Position Fingering

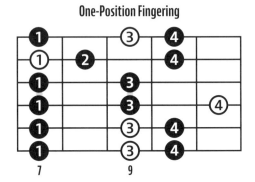

Upper-Diagonal Fingering

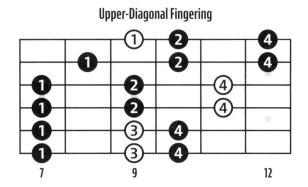

One-Position Intervals

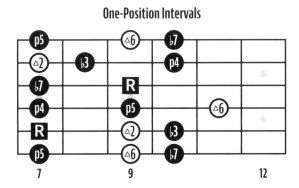

Upper-Diagonal Intervals

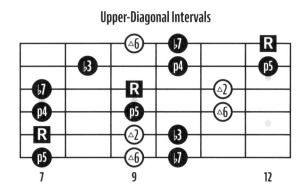

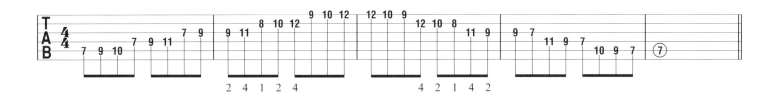

Descending Cells in C Dorian

Play the cell as written, then move it to the new tonal center using the indicated fret number as your guide. Apply a rhythm from below or from the Appendix. Use the scale diagrams and corresponding audio track to change keys. Continue playing the rhythm and improvise your note choices using these backing tracks: C Blues Backing Track 399 for Rhythm 1, D Dorian Backing Track 405 for Rhythm 2, E Dorian Backing Track 409 for Rhythm 3, and G Dorian Backing Track 411 for Rhythm 4.

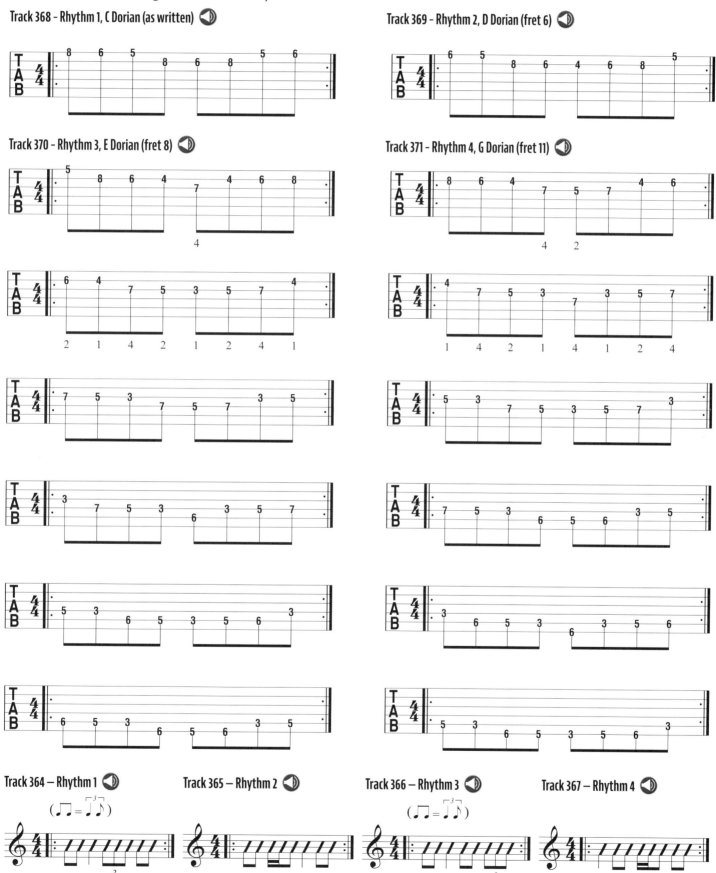

Track 368 - Rhythm 1, C Dorian (as written)

Track 369 - Rhythm 2, D Dorian (fret 6)

Track 370 - Rhythm 3, E Dorian (fret 8)

Track 371 - Rhythm 4, G Dorian (fret 11)

Track 364 – Rhythm 1

Track 365 – Rhythm 2

Track 366 – Rhythm 3

Track 367 – Rhythm 4

145

Ascending Cells in D Dorian

Play the cell as written, then move it to the new tonal center using the indicated fret number as your guide. Apply a rhythm from below or from the Appendix. Use the scale diagrams and corresponding audio track to change keys. Continue playing the rhythm and improvise your note choices using these backing tracks: C Blues Backing Track 399 for Rhythm 1, D Dorian Backing Track 405 for Rhythm 2, E Dorian Backing Track 409 for Rhythm 3, and G Dorian Backing Track 411 for Rhythm 4.

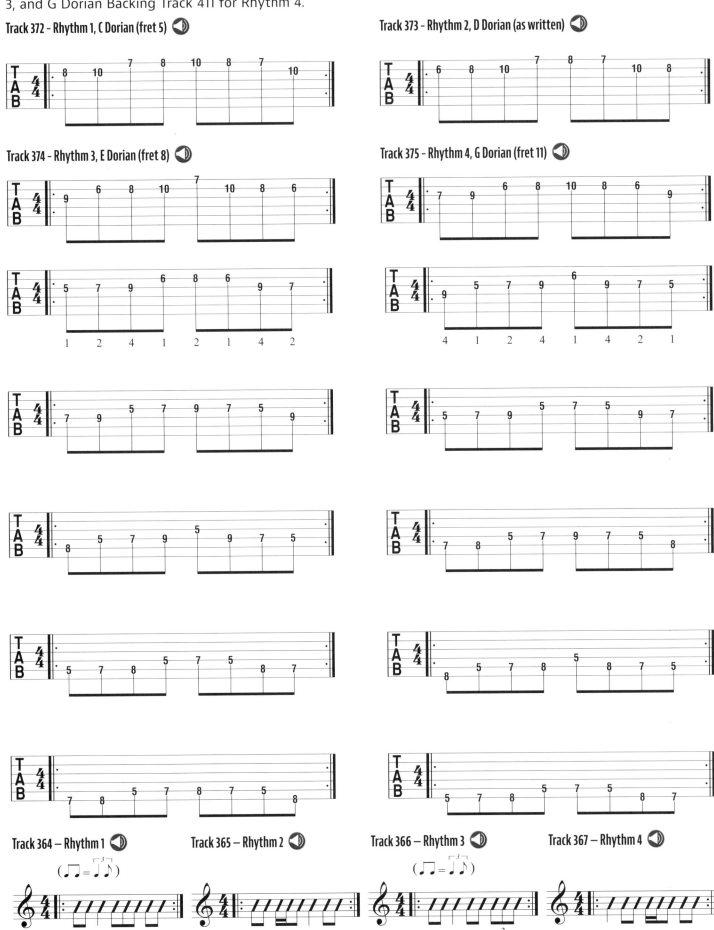

Descending Cells Connected in E Dorian

Track 376 - Rhythm 3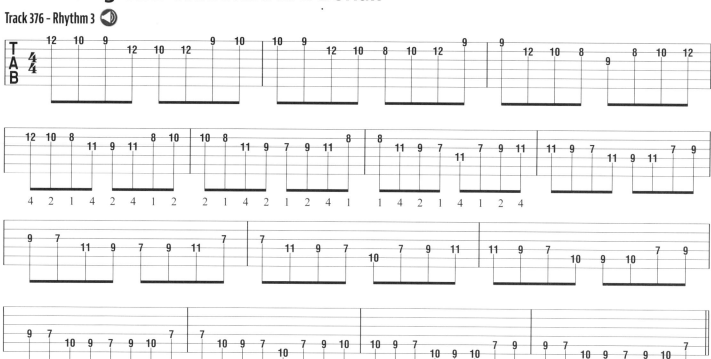

Ascending Cells Connected in G Dorian

Track 377 - Rhythm 4

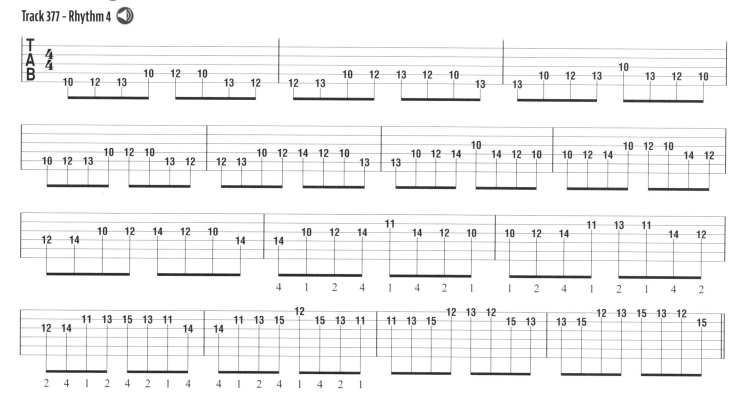

When you can play these easily, take the guide away and use: C Blues Backing Track 399 for Rhythm 1, D Dorian Backing Track 405 for Rhythm 2, E Dorian Backing Track 409 for Rhythm 3, and G Dorian Backing Track 411 for Rhythm 4. More rhythms can be found in the Appendix.

Track 364 – Rhythm 1   Track 365 – Rhythm 2   Track 366 – Rhythm 3   Track 367 – Rhythm 4

Solo 61: C Dorian

Track 378 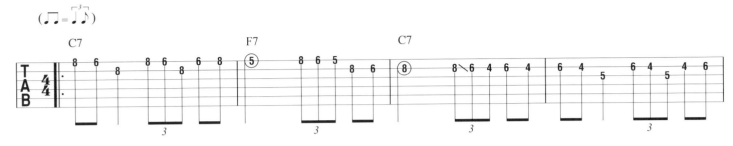   Backing Track 399

Solo 62: D Dorian

Track 379   Backing Track 405

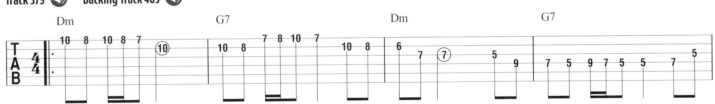

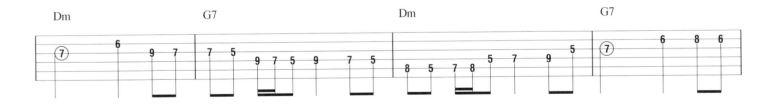

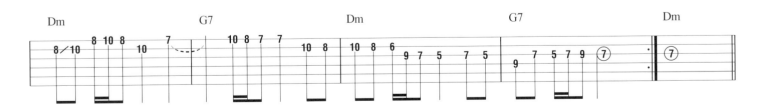

Solo 63: E Dorian

Track 380 Backing Track 409

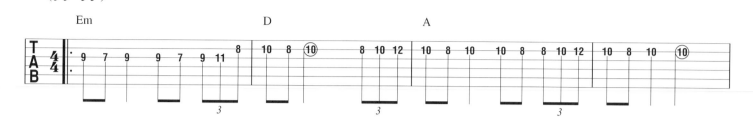

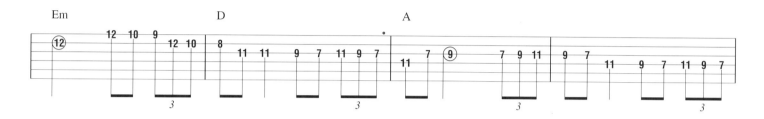

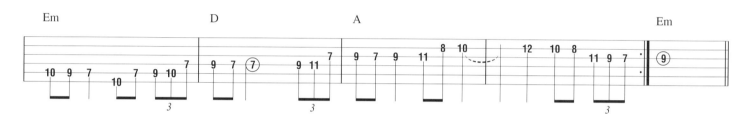

Solo 64: G Dorian

Track 381 Backing Track 411

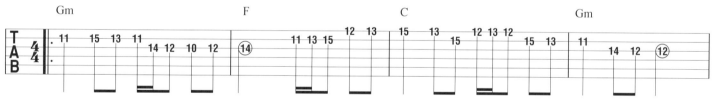

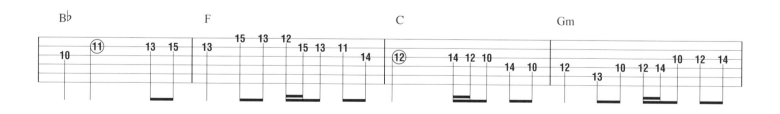

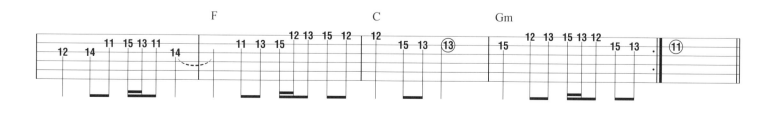

APPENDIX: More Rhythms

Chapter 1: page 10

Chapter 1: page 11

Chapter 1: page 13

Chapter 1: page 14

Chapter 1: page 16

Chapter 1: page 17

Chapter 2: pages 26, 27, 29, 30, 32, and 33

Chapter 3: pages 40 and 41

Chapter 3: page 42

Chapter 3: page 43

Chapter 3: page 45

Chapter 3: page 46

Chapter 4: pages 55, 56, 58, and 59

Chapter 4: pages 61 and 62

Chapter 6: pages 79-81

Chapter 7: pages 85-87

Chapter 8: pages 91-93

Chapter 9: pages 97-99

Chapter 10: pages 103-105

Chapter 11: pages 109-111

Chapter 12: pages 115-117

Chapter 13: pages 121-123

Chapter 14: pages 127-129

Chapter 15: pages 133-135

Chapter 16: pages 139-141

Chapter 17: pages 145-147

ABOUT THE AUTHOR

Since the age of 3-1/2 years old, Kirk Tatnall has been chasing music via his favorite vehicle: the guitar. In addition to authoring instructional books for Hal Leonard, Kirk continues to perform, compose, record, and release original music, teach guitar, and lend his playing to other artists and various commercial music sessions. For more details, please visit **www.kirktatnall.com**.

AUTHENTIC TRANSCRIPTIONS WITH NOTES AND TABLATURE

GUITAR RECORDED VERSIONS®

Guitar Recorded Versions® are note-for-note transcriptions of guitar music taken directly off recordings. This series, one of the most popular in print today, features some of the greatest guitar players and groups from blues and rock to country and jazz.

Guitar Recorded Versions are transcribed by the best transcribers in the business. Every book contains notes and tablature unless otherwise marked. Visit **halleonard.com** for our complete selection.

Will Ackerman
00690016 The Will Ackerman Collection $22.99

Bryan Adams
00690501 Greatest Hits $24.99

Aerosmith
00690002 Big Ones $24.95
00690603 O Yeah! $27.99

Alice in Chains
00690178 Acoustic $19.99
00694865 Dirt $19.99
00660225 Facelift $19.99
00694925 Jar of Flies/Sap $19.99
00690387 Nothing Safe $24.99

All That Remains
00142819 The Order of Things ..$22.99

Allman Brothers Band
00694932 Definitive Collection, Volume 1 ....$27.99
00694933 Definitive Collection, Volume 2 ....$27.99
00694934 Definitive Collection, Volume 3 ....$29.99

Duane Allman
00690958 Guitar Anthology $29.99

Alter Bridge
00691071 AB III $29.99
00690945 Blackbird $24.99
00690755 One Day Remains $24.99

Anthrax
00690849 Best of Anthrax $19.99

Arctic Monkeys
00123558 AM $24.99

Chet Atkins
00690158 Almost Alone $22.99
00694876 Contemporary Styles ..$19.95
00694878 Vintage Fingerstyle $19.99

Audioslave
00690609 Audioslave $24.99
00690884 Revelations $19.95

Avenged Sevenfold
00690926 Avenged Sevenfold $24.99
00214869 Best of: 2005-2013 ..$24.99
00690820 City of Evil $24.95
00123216 Hail to the King $22.99
00691051 Nightmare $22.99
00222486 The Stage $24.99
00691065 Waking the Fallen $22.99

The Avett Brothers
00123140 Guitar Collection $22.99

Randy Bachman
00694918 Guitar Collection $22.95

The Beatles
00690489 1 (Number Ones) $24.99
00694929 1962-1966 ....$24.99
00694930 1967-1970 ....$27.99
00694880 Abbey Road $19.99
00694832 Acoustic Guitar $24.99
00691066 Beatles for Sale $22.99
00690903 Capitol Albums Vol. 2 .$24.99
00691031 Help! $19.99
00690482 Let It Be $19.99
00691030 Magical Mystery Tour ..$22.99
00691067 Meet the Beatles! $22.99
00691068 Please Please Me $22.99
00694891 Revolver $19.99
00691014 Rock Band $34.99
00694914 Rubber Soul $22.99
00694863 Sgt. Pepper's Lonely Hearts Club Band $22.99
00110193 Tomorrow Never Knows $22.99
00690110 White Album Book 1 ..$19.99
00690111 White Album Book 2 ..$19.99
00690383 Yellow Submarine $19.95

The Beach Boys
00690503 Very Best $24.99

Beck
00690632 Beck – Sea Change ...$19.95

Jeff Beck
00691044 Best of Beck $24.99
00691042 Blow by Blow $22.99
00691041 Truth $19.99
00691043 Wired $19.99

George Benson
00694884 Best of $22.99

Chuck Berry
00692385 Chuck Berry $22.99

Billy Talent
00690835 Billy Talent $22.99
00690879 Billy Talent II $19.99

Black Crowes
00147787 Best of $19.99

The Black Keys
00129737 Turn Blue $22.99

Black Sabbath
00690149 Black Sabbath $17.99
00690901 Best of $22.99
00691010 Heaven and Hell $22.99
00690148 Master of Reality $19.99
00690142 Paranoid $17.99
00690145 Vol. 4 ....$22.99
00692200 We Sold Our Soul for Rock 'n' Roll $22.99

blink-182
00690389 Enema of the State $19.95
00690831 Greatest Hits $24.99
00691179 Neighborhoods $22.99

Michael Bloomfield
00148544 Guitar Anthology $24.99

Blue Öyster Cult
00690028 Cult Classics $19.99

Bon Jovi
00691074 Greatest Hits $24.99

Joe Bonamassa
00158600 Blues of Desperation $22.99
00139086 Different Shades of Blue $22.99
00198117 Muddy Wolf at Red Rocks $24.99
00283540 Redemption $24.99

Boston
00690913 Boston $19.99
00690932 Don't Look Back $19.99
00690829 Guitar Collection $24.99

David Bowie
00690491 Best of $19.99

Box Car Racer
00690583 Box Car Racer $19.95

Breaking Benjamin
00691023 Dear Agony $22.99
00690873 Phobia $19.99

Lenny Breau
00141446 Best of $19.99

Big Bill Broonzy
00286503 Guitar Collection $19.99

Roy Buchanan
00690168 Collection $24.99

Jeff Buckley
00690451 Collection $24.99

Bullet for My Valentine
00691047 Fever $22.99
00690957 Scream Aim Fire $22.99
00119629 Temper Temper $22.99

Kenny Burrell
00690678 Best of $22.99

Cage the Elephant
00691077 Thank You, Happy Birthday $22.99

The Cars
00691159 Complete Greatest Hits.$22.99

Carter Family
00690261 Collection $19.99

Johnny Cash
00691079 Best of $22.99

Cheap Trick
00690043 Best of $19.95

Chicago
00690171 Definitive Guitar Collection $24.99

Chimaira
00691011 Guitar Collection $24.99

Charlie Christian
00690567 Definitive Collection ..$22.99

Eric Church
00101916 Chief $22.99

The Civil Wars
00129545 The Civil Wars $19.99

Eric Clapton
00690590 Anthology $34.99
00692391 Best of $22.95
00694896 Blues Breakers (with John Mayall) $19.99
00138731 The Breeze $22.99
00691055 Clapton $22.99
00690936 Complete Clapton $29.99
00690010 From the Cradle $22.99
00192383 I Still Do $19.99
00690363 Just One Night $24.99
00694873 Timepieces $19.95
00694869 Unplugged $24.99
00124873 Unplugged (Deluxe) ..$29.99

The Clash
00690162 Best of $19.99

Coheed & Cambria
00690828 IV $19.95
00139967 In Keeping Secrets of Silent Earth: 3 ....$24.99

Coldplay
00130786 Ghost Stories $19.99
00690593 A Rush of Blood to the Head $19.95

Collective Soul
00690855 Best of $19.95

Jessee Cook
00141704 Works Vol. 1 ....$19.99

Alice Cooper
00691091 Best of $24.99

Counting Crows
00694940 August & Everything After $19.99

Robert Cray
00127184 Best of $19.99

Cream
00694840 Disraeli Gears $24.99

Creed
00288787 Greatest Hits $22.99

Creedence Clearwater Revival
00690819 Best of $24.99

Jim Croce
00690648 The Very Best $19.99

Steve Cropper
00690572 Soul Man $22.99

Crosby, Stills & Nash
00690613 Best of $29.99

Cry of Love
00691171 Brother $22.99

Dick Dale
00690637 Best of $19.99

Daughtry
00690892 Daughtry $19.95

Alex de Grassi
00690822 Best of $19.95

Death Cab for Cutie
00690967 Narrow Stairs $22.99

Deep Purple
00690289 Best of $22.99
00690288 Machine Head $19.99

Def Leppard
00690784 Best of $24.99

Derek and the Dominos
00694831 Layla & Other Assorted Love Songs ..$24.99

Ani DiFranco
00690384 Best of $19.95

Dinosaur Jr.
00690979 Best of $22.99

The Doors
00690347 Anthology $22.95
00690348 Essential Collection ...$16.95

Dream Theater
00160579 The Astonishing $24.99
00122443 Dream Theater $24.99
00291164 Distance Over Time ..$24.99

Eagles
00278631 Their Greatest Hits 1971-1975 ....$22.99
00278632 Very Best of $34.99

Duane Eddy
00690250 Best of $19.99

Tommy Emmanuel
00147067 All I Want for Christmas $19.99
00690909 Best of $24.99
00172824 It's Never Too Late $22.99
00139220 Little by Little $24.99

Melissa Etheridge
00690555 Best of $19.95

Evanescence
00691186 Evanescence $22.99

Extreme
00690515 Pornograffitti $24.99

John Fahey
00150257 Guitar Anthology $19.99

Tal Farlow
00125661 Best of $19.99

Five Finger Death Punch
00691009 5 Finger Death Punch $19.99
00691181 American Capitalism ..$22.99
00128917 Wrong Side of Heaven & Righteous Side of Hell.$22.99

Fleetwood Mac
00690664 Best of $24.99

Flyleaf
00690870 Flyleaf $19.95

Foghat
00690986 Best of $22.99

Foo Fighters
00691024 Greatest Hits $22.99
00691115 Wasting Light $22.99

Peter Frampton
00690842 Best of $22.99

Robben Ford
00690805 Best of $24.99
00120220 Guitar Anthology $29.99

Free
00694920 Best of $19.99

Rory Gallagher
00295410 Blues (Selections) $24.99

Danny Gatton
00694807 88 Elmira St $22.99

Genesis
00690438 Guitar Anthology $24.99

Godsmack
00120167 Godsmack $19.95
00691048 The Oracle $22.99

Goo Goo Dolls
00690943 Greatest Hits Vol. 1 ....$24.99

Grateful Dead
00139460 Guitar Anthology $29.99

Green Day
00212480 Revolution Radio $19.99
00118259 ¡Tré! $21.99
00113073 ¡Uno! $21.99

Peter Green
00691190 Best of $24.99

Greta Van Fleet
00287517 Anthem of the Peaceful Army $19.99
00287515 From the Fires $19.99

Patty Griffin
00690927 Children Running Through $19.95

Guns N' Roses
00690978 Chinese Democracy ...$24.99

Buddy Guy
00691027 Anthology $24.99
00694854 Damn Right, I've Got the Blues $19.95

Jim Hall
00690697 Best of $19.99

Ben Harper
00690840 Both Sides of the Gun .$19.95
00691018 Fight for Your Mind ...$22.99

George Harrison
00694798 Anthology $22.99

Scott Henderson
00690841 Blues Guitar Collection$24.99

Jimi Hendrix
00692930 Are You Experienced? .$27.99
00692931 Axis: Bold As Love $24.99
00690304 Band of Gypsys $24.99
00690608 Blue Wild Angel $24.95
00275044 Both Sides of the Sky $22.99
00692932 Electric Ladyland $27.99
00690017 Live at Woodstock $29.99
00119619 People, Hell & Angels $24.99
00690602 Smash Hits $24.99
00691152 West Coast Seattle Boy (Anthology) $29.99
00691332 Winterland $22.99

H.I.M.
00690843 Dark Light $19.95

Buddy Holly
00660029 Best of $22.99

John Lee Hooker
00690793 Anthology $29.99

Howlin' Wolf
00694905 Howlin' Wolf $22.99

Billy Idol
00690692 Very Best of $22.99

Imagine Dragons
00121961 Night Visions $22.99

Incubus
00690688 A Crow Left of the Murder $19.95

Iron Maiden
00690790 Anthology $24.99
00691058 The Final Frontier $22.99
00200446 Guitar Tab $29.99
00690887 A Matter of Life and Death $24.95

Alan Jackson
00690730 Guitar Collection $29.99

Elmore James
00696938 Master of the Electric Slide Guitar ..$19.99

Jane's Addiction
00690652 Best of $19.95

Jethro Tull
00690684 Aqualung $22.99
00690693 Guitar Anthology $24.99
00691182 Stand Up $22.99

Get Better at Guitar

...with these Great Guitar Instruction Books from Hal Leonard!

101 GUITAR TIPS
INCLUDES TAB

STUFF ALL THE PROS KNOW AND USE

by Adam St. James

This book contains invaluable guidance on everything from scales and music theory to truss rod adjustments, proper recording studio set-ups, and much more.

00695737 Book/Online Audio $16.99

AMAZING PHRASING
INCLUDES TAB

by Tom Kolb

This book/audio pack explores all the main components necessary for crafting well-balanced rhythmic and melodic phrases. It also explains how these phrases are put together to form cohesive solos. The companion audio contains 89 demo tracks, most with full-band backing.

00695583 Book/Online Audio $19.99

ARPEGGIOS FOR THE MODERN GUITARIST
INCLUDES TAB

by Tom Kolb

Using this no-nonsense book with online audio, guitarists will learn to apply and execute all types of arpeggio forms using a variety of techniques, including alternate picking, sweep picking, tapping, string skipping, and legato.

00695862 Book/Online Audio $19.99

BLUES YOU CAN USE

by John Ganapes

This comprehensive source for learning blues guitar is designed to develop both your lead and rhythm playing. Includes: 21 complete solos • blues chords, progressions and riffs • turnarounds • movable scales and soloing techniques • string bending • utilizing the entire fingerboard • and more.

00142420 Book/Online Media..................$19.99

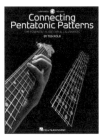

CONNECTING PENTATONIC PATTERNS
INCLUDES TAB

by Tom Kolb

If you've been finding yourself trapped in the pentatonic box, this book is for you! This hands-on book with online audio offers examples for guitar players of all levels, from beginner to advanced. Study this book faithfully, and soon you'll be soloing all over the neck with the greatest of ease.

00696445 Book/Online Audio $19.99

FRETBOARD MASTERY
INCLUDES TAB

by Troy Stetina

Untangle the mysterious regions of the guitar fretboard and unlock your potential. This book familiarizes you with all the shapes you need to know by applying them in real musical examples, thereby reinforcing and reaffirming your newfound knowledge.

00695331 Book/Online Audio $19.99

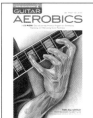

GUITAR AEROBICS
INCLUDES TAB

by Troy Nelson

Here is a daily dose of guitar "vitamins" to keep your chops fine tuned! Musical styles include rock, blues, jazz, metal, country, and funk. Techniques taught include alternate picking, arpeggios, sweep picking, string skipping, legato, string bending, and rhythm guitar.

00695946 Book/Online Audio $19.99

GUITAR CLUES
INCLUDES TAB

OPERATION PENTATONIC

by Greg Koch

Whether you're new to improvising or have been doing it for a while, this book/audio pack will provide loads of delicious licks and tricks that you can use right away, from volume swells and chicken pickin' to intervallic and chordal ideas.

00695827 Book/Online Audio $19.99

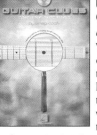

PAT METHENY – GUITAR ETUDES
INCLUDES TAB

Over the years, in many master classes and workshops around the world, Pat has demonstrated the kind of daily workout he puts himself through. This book includes a collection of 14 guitar etudes he created to help you limber up, improve picking technique and build finger independence.

00696587..................$15.99

PICTURE CHORD ENCYCLOPEDIA

This comprehensive guitar chord resource for all playing styles and levels features five voicings of 44 chord qualities for all twelve keys – 2,640 chords in all! For each, there is a clearly illustrated chord frame, as well as *an actual photo* of the chord being played!.

00695224..................$19.99

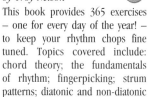

RHYTHM GUITAR 365
INCLUDES TAB

by Troy Nelson

This book provides 365 exercises – one for every day of the year! – to keep your rhythm chops fine tuned. Topics covered include: chord theory; the fundamentals of rhythm; fingerpicking; strum patterns; diatonic and non-diatonic progressions; triads; major and minor keys; and more.

00103627 Book/Online Audio $24.99

SCALE CHORD RELATIONSHIPS
INCLUDES TAB

by Michael Mueller & Jeff Schroedl

This book/audio pack explains how to: recognize keys • analyze chord progressions • use the modes • play over nondiatonic harmony • use harmonic and melodic minor scales • use symmetrical scales • incorporate exotic scales • and much more!

00695563 Book/Online Audio $14.99

SPEED MECHANICS FOR LEAD GUITAR
INCLUDES TAB

by Troy Stetina

Take your playing to the stratosphere with this advanced lead book which will help you develop speed and precision in today's explosive playing styles. Learn the fastest ways to achieve speed and control, secrets to make your practice time really count, and how to open your ears and make your musical ideas more solid and tangible.

00699323 Book/Online Audio $19.99

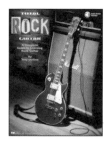

TOTAL ROCK GUITAR
INCLUDES TAB

by Troy Stetina

This comprehensive source for learning rock guitar is designed to develop both lead and rhythm playing. It covers: getting a tone that rocks • open chords, power chords and barre chords • riffs, scales and licks • string bending, strumming, and harmonics • and more.

00695246 Book/Online Audio $19.99

Guitar World Presents STEVE VAI'S GUITAR WORKOUT
INCLUDES TAB

In this book, Steve Vai reveals his path to virtuoso enlightenment with two challenging guitar workouts – one 10-hour and one 30-hour – which include scale and chord exercises, ear training, sight-reading, music theory, and much more.

00119643..................$14.99

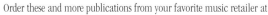

HAL•LEONARD®